SPLENDOR

IN THE

ORDINARY

Splendor in the ORDINARY

BRIAN R. COFFEY

Tyndale House Publishers, Inc.,
Wheaton, Illinois

Library of Congress Cataloging-in-Publication Data

Coffey, Brian R., date
  Splendor in the ordinary / Brian R. Coffey.
    p. cm.
  ISBN 0-8423-5934-6
  1. Bible. N.T. Matthew—Devotional literature. I. Title.
BS2575.4.C64   1993
226.2′06—dc20   92-34955

Printed in the United States of America

99 98 97 96 95 94 93
8   7   6   5   4   3   2

F O R
my father and mother,
ROLAND and JOAN COFFEY,

*whose constant faith and abiding love
became my first glimpse into
the splendor of the King*

ACKNOWLEDGMENTS

Although such words are profoundly inadequate to express the depths of my love for them, I wish to thank my brother Joe and our late youngest brother, John, for their brotherhood, friendship, and the letters and late-night reading sessions from which this book ultimately sprang.

For encouraging me to continue to wrestle with a pile of random thoughts and ideas until they began to take shape, I want to thank my friend Ron Beers, without whom these pages would still be in a drawer in my desk.

Thank you as well to Wightman Weese, my editor, whose suggestions were always gentle and trustworthy.

Heartfelt thanks to the people of First Baptist Church of Geneva, Illinois, for calling and supporting me for six and a half years of ministry; to my colleagues in ministry through those years, Bob Gray, Don Peterson, Mike Nelson, and Dan Baumann, for helping me to grow; and to the hundreds of high school students over the years who have continued to teach me how to teach.

And finally, to my dear and lovely wife, Lorene, and our boys, Jordan and Jesse—thank you all three for filling my days with such joy.

THE UNLIKELY DISCIPLE

He was not an author, although his trade indicates he was literate. He was not a scholar; yet he was bright enough to extort tax money from the poor, cajole bribes from the rich, and do both without getting himself killed by either his Jewish countrymen or their Roman landlords. He was not always even a very good man.

He was Matthew, tax gatherer and sinner by his own admission.

He is also Matthew, sometimes called Levi, apostle and source of the Gospel that bears his name.

We really don't know much about Matthew. He had a whole lot more to say about Peter, James, John, and even Judas, than about himself. We do know he was a Jew, in the service of the Roman conquerors. Most likely he collected on local import and export taxes, a highway toll, or some such levies on which he could overcharge or under-report in such a way as to line his own pockets quite well, thank you. With his integrity, his people, his very soul sold out long ago for gold and silver, Matthew was a despised and distrusted man.

We know that somewhere along the way he had at least two encounters with Jesus of Nazareth. His own sparse description of the events comes to us through the centuries.

> *As Jesus went on from there, he saw a man named Matthew sitting at the tax collector's booth. "Follow me," he told him, and Matthew got up and followed him.*
>
> *While Jesus was having dinner at Matthew's house, many tax collectors and "sinners" came and ate with him and his disciples. When the Pharisees saw this, they asked his disciples, "Why does your teacher eat with tax collectors and 'sinners'?"*
>
> *On hearing this, Jesus said, "It is not the healthy who need a doctor, but the sick. . . . I have not come to call the righteous, but sinners." 9:9-13*

What happened during these two meetings we can only guess. Were they as simple as they sound, or did a rambling yet penetrating conversation wind its way far into the night? We don't know.

We only know that when Matthew got up from that tax booth, when he finally pushed himself away from the table, he followed Jesus into a new life.

Scholars still debate as to how these dog-eared pages made their way from the pen of Matthew to our King James, Revised Standard, New International, or *Living Bible* versions. Did Matthew make original notes in Hebrew based on his eyewitness accounts and memory, making his words the closest we can get to Jesus? Did he use Mark's already extant text and simply amplify it for his unique audience? Did someone else far removed use scraps of data and attribute them to Matthew? No doubt the debate will continue. But if we read the Gospel according to Matthew, there can be no doubt about three things.

First, Matthew wanted us to see Jesus as King. As a Jew, though a backslidden one, Matthew knew his people longed for the rise of a Davidic king to rule their land. Matthew, in nearly every chapter of his Gospel, was trumpeting the good news that a new King had come. But he was a new and different kind of King. Not the kind who humiliates and dominates his subjects, but one who sits down to dinner with them. Not a king who extorts obedience by threat and fear, but one who inspires it by his own love and service. Not a king who kills his enemies, but one who dies in their place. "A new King is here," says Matthew, "his name is Jesus. I know him."

Second, Matthew wanted us to know that this King rules over a new kind of kingdom. A place where the law of the land is not retribution, but forgiveness. Where the currency is not greed, but sacrifice. Where the end is not death, but life. It is called the kingdom of heaven, it belongs to Jesus the King, and the gates are open wide to all who dare to draw near.

Finally, and perhaps most important, both the

King and his kingdom are for ordinary people. The King issues his call, not just to those at the top of the heap, but also to those who feel buried in mediocrity. The King counts as his friends, not just those who have talent and resources to burn, but those who feel they have to overachieve to break even. The kingdom is not just for those who appear to have been born on the doorstep of sainthood, but for those for whom obedience and discipleship is a three-steps-forward, two-steps-back proposition. "The King I know," said Matthew, "doesn't care about who you've been, or who you know, or what you have to offer. He just wants you. Period." Matthew then, I like to imagine, closes with a wry smile, "But I have to warn you, something starts to happen when Jesus gets his hands on ordinary people like me."

You might even call it a miracle.

PART ONE

ORDINARY PEOPLE

CHAPTER ONE

THE FAMILY TREE

*A record of the genealogy of Jesus Christ
the son of David, the son of Abraham:
Abraham was the father of Isaac,
Isaac the father of Jacob,
Jacob the father of Judah and his brothers,
Judah the father of Perez and Zerah,
whose mother was Tamar,
Perez the father of Hezron,
Hezron, the father of Ram,
Ram the father of Amminadab,
Amminadab the father of Nahshon,
Nahshon the father of Salmon,
Salmon the father of Boaz,
whose mother was Rahab,
Boaz the father of Obed, whose mother was Ruth,
Obed the father of Jesse
and Jesse the father of King David.
David was the father of Solomon,
whose mother had been Uriah's wife, . . .
and Jacob the father of Joseph, the husband
of Mary, of whom was born Jesus,
who is called Christ.*

1:1-16

Ordinary. Lately you've had the depressing sensation that your life is far too ordinary. Everywhere you look—magazines, TV, even across the neighborhood—other people are living vibrant, colorful lives, while you plod along in shades of gray and beige.

Do you know the feeling? Your house is gray. You wear gray suits. Others tool around in sleek, new-model cars, while you rattle around in something that looks more appropriate behind a tow truck. Splurging for dessert means a scoop of low-fat, no-cholesterol, vanilla ice cream.

Oh sure, you are busy, what with kids to take to little league and ballet, grass to be cut, and a basement to refinish. Plenty of business, but a tad too ordinary. When you were a kid, you wanted to be a fireman, an astronaut, a circus performer, second baseman for the Yankees, anything but ordinary.

"Ordinary" has quietly tiptoed up and captured your spiritual life as well. You didn't hear it coming. You weren't aware of the precise moment it slipped into the pew seat next to you. But you haven't picked up your Bible in months, you've taken to nodding off before the preacher's third point in the sermon outline, and your prayer life seems to be under siege by some radar-jamming device.

Just the other day you heard a speaker talk about
the importance of disciplined, in-depth Scripture
study for the Christian life, and you felt more than a
twinge of guilt. You decided right then and there to
jump start your spiritual life by reading through the
New Testament.

You find your Bible under a pile of *Time* magazines, junk mail, and week-old newspapers, settle
into your favorite reading chair, and determine to
read at least one full chapter your very first day.

You flip through the tissue-thin pages in reverent
anticipation. "The New Testament," the calligraphy
boldly proclaims—the new thing God has revealed
to humankind. You sincerely long for a dramatic
experience of some such revelation on the personal
level.

At first glance you are disappointed. Chapter 1,
verse 1 of the greatest story ever told—and it begins
with a bone-dry, seemingly pointless recitation of an
ancient family tree. In the very first paragraph your
worst fears about reading the Bible are realized.
Names you can't pronounce, and enough "begats"
to boggle your brain. Meaning so shrouded you
might as well be reading ancient hieroglyphics. Our
voyage through holy writ threatens to be scuttled
on the dry beach of Amminadab, Jeconiah, and
Zadok.

Then, just as we are nodding off like so many
elders on Sunday morning, we notice the names of
five women tucked neatly away in the patriarchal
lineage. Just the fact that these women are even men-

tioned in the male-dominated world of Matthew is
enough to raise our interest. Who they were is
enough to raise our eyebrows.

Take a look. Each of these five women—Tamar,
Rahab, Ruth, Bathsheba (Uriah's wife), and Mary—
had managed, in one way or another, to establish
rather spotty (some would say downright shady)
reputations.

Tamar seduced her own father-in-law (Genesis
38). Rahab was called a harlot (Joshua 2). Ruth
was a foreigner from Moab, Israel's archenemy,
whose appearance in this list would constitute an
embarrassment (book of Ruth). Bathsheba didn't
seem to put up much of an argument when David
made her the object of his lust (2 Samuel 11). And
more than a few fingers must have wagged in
Mary's direction when she was found to be with
child without a husband.

Why, we wonder, does Matthew choose to
include these women in his *Who's Who* of Jesus'
ancestors? Why is it necessary to mention these
women as he introduces us to the King of kings?
Certainly he could have selected better pedigree.
After all, Luke managed to put together a different
and more respectable list.

Perhaps a clue can be found by peeling back the
pages of our own family album. There, preserved
behind sticky plastic sheets, are the grainy black-
and-white faces, some grim and others gay, that constitute the prologue of our lives. As much as we may
or may not like to admit it, we are the product of

generations of people, both noble and common,
whose blood, for better or worse, courses through
our veins.

My ancestry on my mother's side can be traced
through the hills of eastern Kentucky to my grand-
father Noah Sloane. "Pop" had brothers named
Dan, Alec, Wiley, Ples, Lark, Jeff, and Harlan, and
sisters named Arizona and Derona (Arizona wound
up marrying a man named Canada, making her—
you got it—Arizona Canada). My grandmother's
name was Nevajo. They were mountain people,
pure and simple. They worked in coal mines and
general stores. Ordinary folks. Their only claim to
fame was a distant relative (on my Grandmother
Nevajo's side) named Clifton, who had the distinc-
tion of being the last man hanged in Virginia. The
story goes that he shot a man in a feud. His last
request was for his guitar. "Ol' Clifton sang a little
tune," they said, "then they hanged him." In consid-
ering my heritage, the word *royalty* does not easily
come to mind.

My guess is your family closet may hold a secret
or two of its own that you could tell about. Nothing spectacular—just ordinary, run-of-the-mill skeletons hanging there in the dark. Chances are one of
them might involve alcoholism that has skewed relationships in your family for years and robbed you
of peace and hope. Or perhaps there lurks some
form of abuse, the distant voices still attacking your
self-esteem. A broken relationship here, an imma-
ture teenage mistake there. We all have them—

secrets, skeletons, family trees with broken limbs. So did Jesus.

I think Matthew had his reasons for airing this kind of genealogical dirty laundry. He may have been anticipating the response to what had to have been a scandal in its day—the claim to virgin birth. Surely more than a few verbal sticks and stones were hurled in Mary's direction. "Tramp!" they must have whispered over backyard fences. More than once, one can presume, Jesus might have overheard the word *illegitimate* (or worse) in furtive whispers as he walked through the small town of Nazareth.

Have you ever heard those voices? The ones that say, "You've messed up one too many times to be of any good to God or anyone else," or "You've fallen down so often you might as well stay down!" or "Look at yourself; you're just so . . . *ordinary.*"

It just may be that Matthew began his Gospel with this family tree because he wanted folks to know—more than anything else—that God is in the business of taking what the world sees as ordinary failure and redeeming it to accomplish his holy purposes. Our God revels in rolling up his sleeves and taking regular, ordinary, unseemly folks like you and me and redeeming us—failures, disappointments, flawed family trees and all—making us into new creations, fit for his glorious kingdom.

Matthew, after all, should know. An ordinary, despised tax collector, he found himself with a personal invitation to share life with the one he would later call King.

You're still in your easy chair. You've only read seventeen verses. It's already time to put on your ordinary gray coat, jump into your ordinary beige car, and drive to your ordinary job.

Did you hear a clap of thunder as you stumbled over that long list of Hebrew names?

No.

Did you get what you expected from Matthew?

No.

But are you disappointed?

Not a bit!

What Matthew gave you, as you back out of the garage, was the assurance that ordinary people are the raw material God uses for building his kingdom. Read that again. Slowly: *Ordinary people are the raw material God uses for building his kingdom.*

And for that, heaven knows, you and I both qualify. If God can reach into the ordinary lives of Tamar, Rahab, and Bathsheba to give the world a Savior, then he can surely slap the clay of your life on his potter's wheel and mold a vessel that will one day be fit for the King's table.

In fact, Matthew wants us to see that ordinary people may very well be God's favorite kind of clay.

CHAPTER TWO

TWELVE NAMES

*He called his twelve disciples to him
and gave them authority to drive out evil spirits
and to heal every disease and sickness.
These are the names of the twelve apostles: first,
Simon (who is called Peter) and his brother
Andrew; James son of Zebedee, and his brother
John; Philip and Bartholomew; Thomas and
Matthew the tax collector; James son of Alphaeus,
and Thaddaeus; Simon the Zealot and Judas
Iscariot, who betrayed him.*

10:1-4

"**A**ckerman!"

"Here."

"Anderson!"

"Here."

"Brubaker!"

"Here."

"Coffey!"

"Here."

"Mr. Coffey, I can't hear you!"

"HERE!"

Roll call, fifth grade. The sound of my name sends a burning flush from my ears to my armpits. Fifth grade can be brutal. Heaven help you if something about you creates an opportunity for a nickname.

Have you ever had a nickname, or been called a name?

Was it the color of your hair?

Your skinny legs?

Your weight?

It can be anything. For me it was my name, Coffey. For fifth graders it was irresistible and I knew it.

"Maxwell House."

"Coffee cup."

"Coffee Bean."

You name it, I heard it.

You have a name too. Joe. John. Peggy. Elaine. Say your name aloud to yourself right now. What do you feel? Our names usually embarrass us in some small way—perhaps because in some small way our names are us—like it or not. When our names are spoken, we are thrust into the spotlight for all the world to see. When someone knows our name, they know something about us. They wield a certain power. They can speak it and make us pay attention. They can remember it and make us human. They can mispronounce or forget it and make us disappear. They can make fun of it and make us feel like crying.

Names.

I noticed something new this time in Matthew chapter 10, the commissioning of the twelve disciples. In the thick of the granting of power to heal, the instructions for preaching and travel, the marching orders from the Master himself, I noticed the names.

Twelve names.

They don't really need to be there, do they? These men are just extras—sideline players—for most of the gospel story. Surely it would suffice, and save papyrus space, to simply refer to them with a collective, generic term—*disciples,* or *the Twelve,* or *one of the Twelve.* But there they are, twelve names.

We are just as likely, when we speak of the Twelve, to get a kind of polished-marble impression. We imagine St. Peter's in Rome; Michelangelo; the disciples, eyes blank with a statue's otherworldly stare, bodies fixed in some rigid gesture of blessing.

Yet they were not statues, but men. Men with names; names like Simon, who was nicknamed Peter (the Rock), and Andrew, his brother. James and John, the sons of Zebedee. And what about those less famous ones, like Thaddeus, Philip, and Bartholomew? They had names too. Sons and friends, brothers and fathers.

Names.

Between the ages of fourteen and twenty-one, my life was defined pretty much by the confines of a basketball court. During these years I spent count-less hours perfecting crossover dribbles and jump shots over imaginary opponents. Guys like "Pistol" Pete Maravich and Jerry West were my heroes. I spent the night of my senior prom shooting baskets by myself (it helped that I didn't have a date). All those hours paid off when, as a walk-on player, I earned a basketball scholarship at a fine college. My dreams had come true! I was a scholarship ball player. I was somebody.

I soon discovered there were a lot more somebod-ies out there. I continued practicing and playing just as hard—but never made the starting five. For four years I was a second teamer, a scrub, a perennial bench-warmer. But still I was on the team, and I had my scholarship. I was somebody.

At the outset of fall workouts my senior year we were told we'd be getting new practice uniforms. To our delight, we learned our new shorts were to be personally embroidered. I'd seen other college athletes during the summer wearing shorts like this and I had envied them. Now we'd have them too. I would really be somebody.

The day came. I picked up my bag of new workout gear and hurriedly grabbed the shorts, itching to see my name, COFFEY, proudly stitched onto the bright red fabric for the world to see. To my horror, what I saw on those beautiful new practice shorts was COFFEE. After four years and all those practices, all the sweat given for the old home team— now this!

Coffee. Like some freeze-dried powder, or a bag of beans in the supermarket.

I wasn't a starter, I figured. That was why. *I bet none of the stars had their names misspelled,* I thought, moping. But me, a bench-warmer, who cares? I was a nobody.

Ever been there? Passed up for that promotion in favor of the guy who nearly sprained his lips tooting his own horn. The pastor of the church you've attended faithfully for years shakes your hand, looks at you with blank eyes, and says, "Good to see you, uh . . . friend!" You know he hasn't the foggiest idea who you are.

Passed over.

Forgotten.

The message is clear.

"You're not important . . . you're nobody."

Jesus called the Twelve by name. He knew them—

Matthew, Simon the Zealot, Judas, every last one.
When he called their names he remade them as
men, from fishermen to fishers of men, from
crooked tax collector to straight-shooting Gospel
writer.

Jesus knows my name too, and yours. He gets it
right every time. He knows me, and to him I am
somebody. You are too.

Say your name again. This time imagine Jesus
saying it to you. It is by our names that Jesus calls
us.

Listen! Can you hear him?

CHAPTER THREE

MIRACLE IN A SACK LUNCH

*The crowds followed him on foot
from the towns. When Jesus landed
and saw a large crowd, he had
compassion on them and healed their sick.
As evening approached, the disciples came to him
and said, "This is a remote place, and it's already
getting late. Send the crowds away, so they can go
to the villages and buy themselves some food."
Jesus replied, "They do not need to go away.
You give them something to eat."
"We have here only five loaves of bread
and two fish," they answered.
"Bring them here to me," he said. And he directed
the people to sit down on the grass. Taking the five
loaves and the two fish and looking up to heaven,
he gave thanks and broke the loaves. Then he gave
them to the disciples, and the disciples gave them to
the people. They all ate and were satisfied, and the
disciples picked up twelve basketfuls of broken
pieces that were left over. The number of those who
ate was about five thousand men,
besides women and children.*

14:13-21

"Be back by dark!" his mom called after him as he flew out the door and down the walk. "And don't forget your lunch!"

Oh, Mom, he thought, but retraced his steps and grabbed the cloth-wrapped bundle held out through the kitchen window.

"If I know you, you'll be starved by noon—especially if you spend the whole day chasing after that new prophet and his gang. And be careful!"

"Don't worry Mom—I'll be fine," he chirped over his shoulder. It was the last day of summer vacation, and he had coaxed his mother into letting him join the crowds following the new teacher. They said Jesus sometimes did miracles. He knew he probably couldn't get close to him, but just maybe . . . Excitement over this quest for adventure rose in his young heart as he ran.

In the gathering dusk on a Galilean hillside the disciples are dog-tired. People have been coming out of nowhere all day, pressing and pushing, trying to get close to Jesus. It's been twelve against twenty thousand, and they're tired of crowd control. They are up to their bearded chins with runny-nosed children, senior citizens with goiters, and all manner of back ailments. They urge Jesus to send the hungry

crowd into town to eat before everything closes up.
The last thing they wanted to hear was what Jesus
said next.

"They don't have to go away. You give them
something to eat."

Right. The way John tells it, Philip stammers
something like, "Us give them something to eat? A
thousand shekels wouldn't even be a start!" One
can imagine the Twelve looking at each other, hoping the Master was pulling their legs with his outra-
geous suggestion. But when they looked back at
him, they could tell by his face he was dead serious.

Jesus looks out at the crowd, now huddled in desperate little pockets, awaiting their chance to get
close to him. They are hungry, but they will not
budge for fear of losing their opportunity to feel his
touch.

He is moved.

He looks at his disciples. They are, as usual, shoo-
ing people away, trying vainly to get everyone to go
home. When they come and ask for his help, he vol-
leys the ball of responsibility squarely into their
court.

"You see the same needy crowd I do. They're
tired and hungry. But it doesn't appear they'll leave
until we see them all. What are you going to do
about it?"

Don't just stand there, thumbs in pockets, shrug-
ging your shoulders looking helpless. Do something.
Think. Work. Hope.

Can you identify with how the disciples must have
felt? We are bombarded nightly on the six o'clock
news with images of a suffering world. War. Fam-
ine. Poverty. The faces of hungry children and griev-
ing mothers.

So many problems.

So many people.

Ever found yourself saying, "But what can I do?
I'm only one person! Everything I have would just
be a drop of water in an ocean of need!" We're ordinary people with ordinary resources and abilities.
What difference can we possibly make?

Just then another of the disciples bulldozes through
the crowd, a shy-looking boy in tow. With a self-
conscious grin, he holds up the boy's bundled-up
lunch and says in half jest, "Here's a couple of fish
and some bread."

Jesus doesn't smile, but rather looks directly at
the young boy and tells the disciple to bring the
boy's lunch to him.

During the summer of 1982, as a graduate student searching for vocation, I spent seven weeks as
a volunteer intern at a church in inner-city Pittsburgh. Just across a city park from the church was a
very poor, run-down section of town—a ghetto.
Many of the people living there were Hmong refu-
gees, who had fled horrible suffering in Laos only to
find themselves dumped in third-floor, roach-
infested, slum apartments.

Most of my time was spent getting to know the Hmong children, especially the teenagers. We played games, organized a little Bible-story club, and just talked a lot so they could practice their English. Eventually they would invite me to their homes for dinner. It was summer and very hot. The apartments had no air-conditioning, and garbage was piled up behind the buildings.

It was poverty you could smell.

I remember writing a friend about my first experiences there, and I remember his response: "You probably will not change Pittsburgh this summer, but Pittsburgh just might change you."

One night, a couple of weeks after arriving, I was up late reading in the little upstairs room in the church where I stayed, when I noticed what looked like giant fireflies in the park across the street. A dozen lights were slowly bobbing around in the dark. But they were too big to be fireflies, and they moved too slowly to be children playing flashlight tag.

I didn't have a clue why they were there.

After several nights, curiosity got the best of me and I ventured to find out. To my surprise, it was the Hmong women and children, each holding a flashlight and an empty gallon-sized plastic milk container. They were walking stooped over staring intently at the ground. Every few minutes they would bend down, scratch at the dirt, put something in the jug, and continue on.

They were filling their jugs with night crawlers.

Worms.

They had discovered that the bait shops along Pittsburgh's three rivers would pay seven dollars per gallon jug of worms. They were supplementing their family incomes by digging worms.

My last night in Pittsburgh, the Hmong kids and I went to a movie, had a little party, exchanged addresses, and said a sad good-bye. A couple hours later, as I packed my things, I heard a shrill voice calling up from the sidewalk outside the church. "Bdian! . . . Bdian!"

I knew it was one of the Hmong kids. They couldn't pronounce *r*s very well. When I looked down I saw Neng in the glow of the streetlight. He was on his little Stingray bicycle and was wearing his ever-present baseball cap. Neng was fourteen, but he was about the size of an American ten-year-old.

The first time I met him he was playing with the others in the park, hollering out obscene words in English at the top of his lungs. Neng was loud, often angry, and hard to keep under control. It was hard for me to like Neng. But we gradually developed a friendship.

In the process I found that, like many other Hmong, Neng had lived a nightmare childhood. He watched his father executed by the North Vietnamese. He swam across the Mekong River to a refugee camp in Thailand while troops fired bullets into the water. He had been a boat person, convinced he would die.

That night as I walked downstairs I wondered what Neng wanted at 11:30 P.M. As I stepped into the light with him, he pulled a folded envelope out of his back pocket. He gave it to me, hat pulled almost over his eyes, and said, "This is present for you. Maybe you buy some food." Then he turned and pedaled furiously into the night.

I stood there for the longest time, afraid to open the envelope. I knew what was inside.

When I finally did, there was a ten-dollar bill.

Tears rolled down my face, as they often do when I think of it, for I knew what that ten dollars cost my little friend.

A gallon and a half of night crawlers.

For me.

My friend was right. Pittsburgh did change me.

Jesus took that young boy's lunch, gave thanks, and fed five thousand men, besides women and children. Just when we are tempted to think we are too ordinary to have anything to offer, just when we are tempted to think our puny, ordinary lives can't possibly make a difference, Jesus finds a miracle in a sack lunch.

Miracles begin with simple sacrifice.

The boy helped Jesus work a miracle for the crowd of sick and hungry people.

Neng helped Jesus work a miracle in me.

Jesus works the miraculous in and through ordinary people. It is true—we can't change the world by ourselves. Fortunately, we don't have to. We just have to give Jesus what we have. He'll do the rest.

When you're tempted to think you're too ordinary to be of use to Jesus, remember the boy with the sack lunch. The sacrifices of ordinary people, when placed in the hands of Jesus, work miracles.

CHAPTER FOUR

ON BEING SALTY

You are the salt of the earth.
But if the salt loses its saltiness,
how can it be made salty again?

5:13

He was a sophomore in high school, hormones blazing, thinking about what adolescent males think about once every fifteen seconds.

Girls.

This particular fifteen seconds he was thinking about a girl named Jane who had a reputation as being . . . well, easy. At least his buddies said so. So he asked her for a date. One could safely assume his motives were not exactly worthy of sainthood.

His plan was simple. Borrow a car, check out the school dance for a few minutes, then drive to a secluded spot and see if the reputation was true.

At least that was the plan.

To his dismay, no sooner was the parking brake set than she shrugged off his opening move with disinterested firmness. Before he could regroup for a second charge she said, "I think there's something you should know." She then proceeded to tell him she had heard a traveling preacher at a revival in town the previous weekend and had been converted.

She didn't do certain things anymore.

The sophomore boy drove home disappointed, but impressed.

In one of his most well-remembered analogies, Jesus says his followers are the "salt of the earth." Salt was, in his day, a precious commodity used to preserve meat from decay, a mineral necessary for life, a seasoning that added taste.

One can assume it also tended to make folks thirsty.

The sophomore boy didn't call Jane again, but he did think about his experience, or lack thereof, with her that night.

A couple of weeks later two friends from his football squad invited him to attend a revival meeting, and, surprising even himself, he went.

The rest, as they say, is history.

The boy had a powerful conversion experience and by the time he graduated from high school was a licensed preacher. He went on to attend Bible college and a Christian university in Indiana. While there he met a Christian girl named Joan. They married and had three boys. He became a respected pastor within his denomination. Of their three sons, two eventually entered the ministry as well (the third may have too, but he died in an accident at age twenty).

I am that sophomore boy's eldest son.

From one teenage girl with a new commitment to purity to two generations of pastors and thousands of persons touched. I ask you, Is there power in regular old ordinary people being salty? Is this salt a precious commodity? Does this salt preserve the world from corruption?

Christians are just ordinary people with a commitment to purity.

The salt of the earth.

Jesus went on to say we can lose our saltiness. Whatever else he may or may not be saying about eternal security, he is saying that every now and then we should check to see if anyone around us is becoming thirsty.

CHAPTER FIVE

THEY COULD NOT

When they came to the crowd,
a man approached Jesus and knelt before him.
"Lord, have mercy on my son," he said.
"He has seizures and is suffering greatly.
He often falls into the fire or into the water.
I brought him to your disciples, but they
could not heal him."

17:14-16

We watched dumbstruck as the pickup pulled up in a cloud of dust. A twenty-something guy jumped from the cab decked out in full biking regalia. Lycra-spandex biking shorts, neon designer jersey, helmet, gloves—he had it all. He proceeded to grab his twenty-one-speed racing bike from the bed of the truck and wheel it over to the sign that read Hoosier Pass, Elev. 11,582 ft. He posed proudly as his female companion snapped a picture—then they both jumped back into the truck, made a U-turn, and drove down the mountain.

We were incensed.

"Fake."

"Phony."

"Poser!"

We hurled our disgust after the truck now disappearing around the first hairpin turn.

Only moments before, our cycling group, made up mostly of high school students, had completed an eleven-mile climb to the top of the pass. Three and a half hours of pedaling uphill—wondering if we would ever see the top, if the burning in our legs and lungs would ever stop—ended with exultant whoops and shouts as the last riders wobbled to the peak.

It hadn't been pretty.

We had to stop and rest.

Some wanted to quit.

Some had to walk their bikes at the top.

One got sick along the way.

But we made it. And we had just taken our group picture and were still standing around enjoying the camaraderie of the moment when Mr. Hypocrite swaggered up and desecrated our holy ground with his cheap imitation.

I wonder if all of us aren't sometimes a little like the phony biker. Something has convinced us that we must appear to be more than we are, that image is more important than character—or honesty—that image is everything. The photo on our mantle must not be of us huffing and grunting our way up the hill or—heaven forbid—walking our bike because we raised our white flag of exhausted surrender a half mile from the top. No. Our photo has to be of us standing at the summit, smiling, hair perfectly groomed, as if we'd gotten there without breaking a sweat.

Ordinary isn't good enough.

Not by a long shot.

We've got to be superstars.

Admit we are tired of trying so hard? Never. Admit we feel like quitting? No way. Admit we sometimes have trouble mustering the faith to lob one more prayer at the ceiling? Can't do it. Got to keep smiling. Got to keep acting as if we've got this faith thing in the bag, no sweat.

A man, writes Matthew, comes to Jesus begging healing for his disturbed son.

"I brought him to your disciples, but they could not heal him."

They could not.

I find myself identifying strongly with the disciples. So many things we cannot do. For every instance of clearly answered prayer a thousand seem to be put on "hold."

Joachin is an eleven-year-old boy in the Dominican Republic. His legs, looking like twisted pipe cleaners, are folded on the seat of his rickety wheelchair. He has polio.

Sue, a devoted mother, wife, and church leader, has suffered from lupus for thirty years. Doctors have performed nearly twenty operations on her hands and knees alone. She's survived a kidney transplant. A month ago they found lumps in her breasts. She had to have a double radical mastectomy.

Someone is sick, in pain. The story could be repeated a million times. We pray, we touch, we weep, and we pray some more. But we cannot heal them. We feel so powerless. We wonder. We even doubt.

Sometimes we doubt a lot.

Jesus seems to attribute the disciples' failure to smallness of faith.

"If you have faith as small as a mustard seed, you

can say to this mountain, 'Move from here to there' and it will move."

I have struggled long and hard to come to grips with life in a world of pain and suffering. You have too. We have, of necessity, constructed a theology large enough to embrace both a loving God and a world in all its unhealed anguish. We still pray. We still hope. But we don't get our hopes up. God must, we figure, have his own reasons for not healing our dear friend Sue. One day, in heaven we presume, we will know why.

Then Jesus has to go and talk about faith and the mustard seed. He makes it sound as if any knucklehead could, easy as pie, make Joachin's legs stout as stove pipes. What gives?

But Jesus also says a few other things.

"Bring him here to me."

"Come to me all you who are weary and tired. . . ."

"Don't be like the hypocrites—who stand and pray flowery prayers to be seen as religious superstars. No, go alone to your private place and pour your heart out to Jesus. The Father knows what you need."

The disciples failed.

At the very moment they needed the faith that moves mountains, it crumbled like a stale cookie.

When their faith needed to be of the superstar variety, it came up ordinary.

They could not heal the boy.

But you have to give them credit, as I suppose
Jesus did as well. At least they came to the right
place with their failure.

"Bring him here to me," Jesus said.

And they did.

I believe in Jesus, and I suspect you do too. I have
faith, although I suspect that far too often my faith
is far smaller than a mustard seed.

I pray for the people I love. Sometimes their suffering is relieved. Most of the time it is not.

Sometimes it gets worse.

My faith sometimes tells me God has the power
to heal, to move mountains, to raise friends from
the dead any old time he wants.

Sometimes my faith is very weak.

But that day the disciples discovered one thing
that I desperately need to know. They found that
even when their faith was ordinary, they could
always come to Jesus.

When they could not do a blessed thing, he could.

When we cannot muster up mustard-seed faith,
he can.

When our faith melts into failure, when our leap
of faith runs smack-dab into the wall of doubt,
Jesus says, "Bring it here to me."

Jesus is not afraid of our ordinary faith. He does
not require us to be mountain-moving superstars
before we can come to him. He is interested not
only at the triumph of the summit, but also when
the road seems longest and most steep.

It is true that one day our faith will be made

sight. But for now, times will come, as they did for the Twelve, when we feel unable to muster the faith to look at the mountain—let alone move it. In those tired and ordinary times, remember these words: "Bring him here to me."

CHAPTER SIX

RANDY

*"Again, it will be like a man going on a journey,
who called his servants and entrusted his property
to them. To one he gave five talents of money, to
another two talents, and to another one talent,
each according to his ability. Then he went on his
journey. The man who had received the five talents
went at once and put his money to work and
gained five more. So also, the one with the two
talents gained two more. But the man who had
received the one talent went off, dug a hole in the
ground and hid his master's money."*

25:14-18

Whomp! Randy fell on his face in the Mexican dirt.

When Randy fell, he fell hard. And he fell a lot. He would catch his crutch in a crevice or on a stone, and down he would go. Because his hands were preoccupied with crutches and his legs useless, he would fall forward with nothing to break his fall but his face. He'd grin his sheepish, gap-toothed grin and say something like, "That was about a 9.5," as a companion helped him up.

Randy had cerebral palsy.

At twenty-five years of age, even the simplest physical task required tremendous effort and concentration. Lurching forward with a tortuous gait, Randy looked like a marionette controlled by a drunken puppeteer. Knees locked together, he used his arm crutches to drag his feet viciously along half behind, half underneath him. His shoulders looked as if they would explode from their sockets with the strain.

You could hear Randy coming from half a block away—the distinctive scraping sound, punctuated by the *thump* of his crutches stabbing at the dusty ground.

The walkways on the work site were rutted, rock-encrusted, dirt paths. Every time the work team walked from the dorms to the main building or to the fields, someone had to walk with Randy. The group was in Mexico to work on an agricultural project for a Third World development organization. The work was hard: digging crop terraces and irrigation ditches. Hoeing weeds out of fields of corn and beans. Mixing concrete for the construction of classrooms and latrines. The conditions were primitive, including a fifty-yard walk through those same rutted paths to use the outhouse.

But Randy was there, crutches, lurching, kamikaze-style walk and all.

The others couldn't help but wonder why he'd come. He couldn't do most of the work. It took him ten minutes or more each way just to get to the fields. He was in real danger of hurting himself falling on that hard ground. This was no place for someone like Randy.

Good thing no one told Randy.

He spent most of the twelve days sitting in a clearing a little way from where the others swung their picks in the raw field. He put seeds into little bags of soil. Seed by seed. Bag by bag. Flies and gnats buzzing unmolested around his head, sweaty smudges of dirt on his face from his last fall, he prepared hundreds of these little bags to be planted in the trenches the others were digging.

One day they were startled to see Randy struggling toward the field dragging a chair with him.

"Now what's he doing?"

"He's going to kill himself!"

"The guy just doesn't know when to quit."

"He can't work out here!"

Good thing no one told Randy.

With a little help, he sat in the chair at the edge of a fresh irrigation ditch and asked for a pick. He was tired, he said, of just doing the bags of seeds. He wanted to dig.

"Randy, you can't be doing that."

"You're going to hurt yourself."

"Come on, let's go back to doing the seeds—it's safer."

He was insistent. "I want to dig."

And so he did. Sitting in his chair, he took the pick, and the grin worked its way across his face again. His first couple of hacks at the earth were tentative as he tried to gauge his balance. He didn't move much soil. Randy frowned. He didn't like not moving any dirt. His arms were remarkably strong from years of supporting the dead weight of his lower body, and soon he was swinging the pick for all he was worth. Grunting with each mighty effort, he wielded his weapon like a deranged samurai warrior.

It was inevitable.

They were all afraid it would happen.

With one mighty swing that missed its mark, Randy flung himself headlong out of his chair and wound up a crumpled wreck in the ditch.

"Randy!?"

"Someone get him out of there!"

"You OK?"

"Why are you doing this?"

Back on his chair, dirt clods clinging to his shirt, a scrape on his arm oozing blood, but still holding his pick with both hands, Randy said with a goofy grin, "I just wanna serve Jesus. I'm having fun!"

The kingdom of heaven, says Jesus, is like the man who, before departing on a long journey, left his assets with his servants.

You know the story.

It was like winning the state lottery. To one wide-eyed servant the boss gave a thousand shares of the Fortune 500 company. To another he gave twice that amount. To the third a full five thousand shares.

We're talking "Wheel of Fortune."

Big money.

The most surprising thing to the servants must have been that there were seemingly no strings attached. No explanation. No instructions of what was expected. No threats. No complicated fine print about buying low and selling high. Just, "I'm going away for a while. I've given each of you what I think you can handle. See you later."

You know what happened next.

The servant given five talents "went at once and put his money to work and gained five more." The one with two gained two more. Maybe they bought an olive grove and had a good crop. Maybe they bought up a couple of two-flats and took in some rental income. Maybe they started a restaurant.

Whatever they did, their invested shares got a 100-percent return. Not too shabby.

The last fellow was a bit more conservative. Knowing his boss to be pretty tough on the bottom line, he stuffed the notes in his mattress and sweated out the nights until the big guy came back.

The boss returned.

You know the rest of the story.

He calls each of the servants before his mahogany desk to settle up. The one with five returns ten and gets a big-time slap on the back.

"Well done my boy. You've got quite a future. Whaddaya say to a lifetime partnership?"

The second servant brings in four where he had two. Same response.

The third servant lays his one talent, rumpled and smelling of mildew, on the desk and says, "At least I didn't lose anything."

"What did you say?"

"At least I didn't lose anything. I kept your money safe."

"Didn't LOSE anything!? Didn't LOSE ANYTHING!? Of course you lost something. Ever heard of a bank? How 'bout a CD? You could have at least gained a few pennies interest! Yes, you have lost something. You lost an opportunity. You lost the opportunity of a lifetime."

Before leaving the office he left a memo for his secretary. "Have one more talent added to the top account."

I don't know about you, but I have always felt

the third servant got a bit of a raw deal. I mean, he was right, wasn't he? The others could have lost their shirts. Then what? The old man would have had their hides. With the banks like they are, who can trust them?

He played it safe.

He didn't lose anything.

He didn't risk anything.

Yes sir! I've always identified with that third servant. I've always thought he got a raw deal.

Until I met Randy.

Somewhere in rural southwestern Mexico there is a field full of corn and beans. That corn and those beans help provide nutrition for a whole town of Mexican peasants and their children. That corn and those beans are there because a guy named Randy sat stuffing seeds into little cellophane bags. The ditch that irrigates that field is there because a guy named Randy threw himself into it while digging it.

Randy didn't have five talents.

He wasn't given two.

Some would argue he didn't even have one.

But what Randy had he invested. Crutches, goofy grin, and all, Randy threw himself into serving Jesus with reckless abandon. He didn't care how he looked. He didn't care if he fell on his face. He didn't care if all his picking left him sprawled in a ditch. He just wanted to serve Jesus.

You know what? I believe Randy does have fun.

And I believe God has fun watching.

CHAPTER SEVEN

AT A DISTANCE

*"Lord, if it's you," Peter replied, "tell me to come
to you on the water." "Come," he said. Then Peter
got down out of the boat, walked on the water and
came toward Jesus. But when he saw the wind, he
was afraid and, beginning to sink, cried out,
"Lord, save me!"*

14:28-30

*"But what about you?" he asked. "Who do you
say I am?" Simon Peter answered, "You are the
Christ, the Son of the living God."*

16:15-16

*"I tell you the truth," Jesus answered, "this very
night, before the rooster crows, you will disown me
three times." But Peter declared, "Even if I have to
die with you, I will never disown you."*

26:34-35

After a little while, those standing there went up to Peter and said, "Surely you are one of them, for your accent gives you away." Then he began to call down curses on himself and he swore to them, "I don't know the man."

26:73-74

The man snipping away at my head had sweat stains at his armpits and hair protruding from his nostrils. Sitting in the high-backed barber chair, trying valiantly but in vain to dodge his latest volley of inane pass-the-time questions, I wanted nothing more than to be left to the solitude of my sports magazine. No such luck. Looking over my shoulder, the curious barber piped up, "How 'bout those Cubs? Sure, they're winnin' now, but you just wait. They'll find some way to mess it up. Always do."

Snip. Snip.

"So whaddaya do, anyway?"

Having never been in his shop before, I had no idea what kind of man wielded the scissors poking around my ears. But he didn't seem the Christian or religious type. I had noticed a *Playboy* magazine on top of his stack of reading material as I waited my turn. His language was not offensive, but salty enough. I was a part-time youth pastor and full-time seminary student, doing neither particularly well, now suddenly trapped with this curious heathen barber wrist-deep in my hair. Presented with a golden opportunity to bear witness, though in a small way, to the one in whom I had found life and

meaning, I, the seminary student and aspiring minister, went cold down to my toes.

"I'm a student," I said, not entirely untruthfully,
and flipped the page.

I left the barbershop that day with a nice enough
haircut, but with a heart full of questions. Why,
when I stood weekly before my fledgling youth
group of twenty half-listening high school students
and boldly proclaimed the gospel, could I not even
bring myself to admit my vocation to a total
stranger? What had embarrassed me so much about
the barber's question? How could I fail to acknow-
ledge Jesus, whom I serve, at such a harmless and
opportune moment?

Have you ever found yourself in those shoes? Someone asks an innocent question, or a conversation
takes a sudden spiritual detour, and voila! You have
a golden opportunity to become a witness for
Christ, a light shining in darkness.

It might be with a few coworkers over lunch or
by the copy machine.

It might be with the guys after a pickup game of
basketball.

Maybe it's with a family member who has let his
or her spiritual life slide.

Whatever the situation, it was right there. You
know what could have been said, maybe even what
should have been said but, like me, you slithered
out of the spotlight with a nifty sidestep.

Why do we do it?

Maybe it's because something about following Jesus sounds a little odd in our microchip, laser-disk world. To believe at all seems quaint and irrelevant, let alone to make a public spectacle of it or, in my case, a career of such belief.

Maybe I'm afraid of feeling foolish.

Maybe I fear being unable to answer questions that might come.

Maybe I fear being considered quaint or irrelevant.

Maybe you do, too.

If you never have found yourself feeling like a failure in the share-your-faith department, you can just skip ahead to the next chapter. But if you have, I invite you to take a look with me at Matthew's portrayal of our patron saint—Peter, of course.

In the verses at the beginning of this chapter, we read four dramatic statements delivered in four very different circumstances of Peter's life.

"Lord, save me!"

"You are the Christ!"

"I'll never disown you!"

"I don't even know the man!"

One man. Four declarations. All completely transparent expressions of man struggling to follow Jesus. From the desperate gurgle of a drowning man, to the courageous recognition of truth; from the white-hot fires of commitment, to the shame of total denial. Peter's life, sometimes triumphant, sometimes tragic, is splattered all over Matthew's Gospel.

Why Peter? Why not Bartholomew? Or Thaddeus? We know next to nothing about those guys. Matthew gives us only the slightest peek at his own life. But Peter, oh, our dear impulsive, on-again, off-again Simon Peter—he's right there for us to point fingers at, laugh at, learn from, and love.

Peter seems to be the disciple about whom we are told the most because he is the one with whom we can identify the most. He is capable of great insight and heart-pounding courage, but also of choking fear and downright betrayal.

Peter is just an ordinary guy learning to follow Jesus.

He took a lot of bumps and bruises and made many wrong turns on his way from the one mending fisherman's nets to becoming the one called Saint Peter. Most of us are somewhere on that road ourselves.

Take a look at Peter, you might see someone you know.

The seas have turned nasty. Waves hammer their boat, and the wind drives spray like nails into their raw faces. They've seen it before. But never like this. They are in trouble. Peter, for all his blustering machismo and seafaring skill, is afraid.

Matthew tells us they've battled the gale all night long when, near morning, they see what they first think is a ghost. It's not a ghost, of course, but Jesus, coming to them on the water.

Peter, whether motivated by faith in Jesus or fear of his boat becoming an underwater tomb should he stay put, goes overboard for Jesus. Unable to outrun his fear, he finds himself up to his armpits in seaweed, exhausted, and sinking fast. He croaks what must be among the most unself-conscious and honest prayers ever uttered, "Lord, save me!"

The journey of the disciple, Peter found, begins at the end. The winds were fierce, the waves high, and he felt himself sinking in the storm. He has nothing left with which to keep himself afloat—no boat, no ropes, not even a handy inflatable life vest. He is at the end of his strength. The end of his resources and skill. The end of his considerable self-reliance and courage. Confronted by the end, he stretches a wet hand toward Jesus, "Lord, save me!"

Although most of us aren't quite so melodramatic about it, becoming a Christian is about going overboard for Jesus. Whether we are sinking in a storm-filled life, or simply watching our life slip away like sand through a sieve, we recognize we are at the end.

We can no longer ignore the guilt we carry around like a backpack full of rocks.

We can no longer deny that we think about death.

We have grown weary of the constant effort of building flimsy facades for our lives, weary of acting happy when we aren't, trying to believe we're in control when everything is coming apart. We long

to let go, to throw ourselves into the dark sea of
faith, and find the strong hand that can hold us
afloat.

And he is there.

"Who do people say the Son of Man is?" Jesus
asked, nodding toward the disciples without taking
his eyes from his bowl.

They stop chewing their lunch and glance side-
ways at each other like junior high boys who didn't
do their homework.

"Uh, some say John the Baptist—or Elijah."

"Someone asked me if you were Jeremiah come
back to life."

"Most everybody thinks you're a prophet."

"But what about you?" He scanned the faces of
his fidgety friends until his eyes fell on Peter. "Who
do you say that I am?"

The others, having avoided eye contact with Jesus
by picking at the ground, or staring intently at the
backs of their hands, were now relieved to have the
spotlight on Peter. They waited for him to speak.

Peter didn't look down; he didn't fidget. He just
looked hard at Jesus for the longest time. When he
finally spoke, those who knew him well could
detect a hint of tears on the rims of his eyes.

"You are the Christ," Peter said in a voice none
of them had heard before, "the Son of the living
God."

Peter's confession went beyond the desperate,
"Lord save me!" of a drowning man. Identifying

Jesus as the Christ, the Messiah, while every bit as loony as jumping out of a boat into a thrashing sea, is the measured and intentional response of a man who knows Jesus. Not just a man looking for salvation, but a man who has found his Savior.

Yes, it starts at the end. It begins with going overboard. But soon we find so much more. As a newborn babe, we have so much more to learn. We are saved. Our hearts have found rest in his great hands. But we must learn to stand, to walk, to see, to speak.

The path of the disciple passes through the question, Who do you say that I am?

As a child you had a hero. FDR, Joe DiMaggio, Ike, Mickey Mantle, Elvis. Maybe you also dreamed of one day becoming a hero. Scoring a last-second touchdown, hitting a ninth-inning homer, discovering a cure for cancer, rescuing a frail victim from the clutches of the school bully, becoming a missionary to China. You longed to "march into hell for a heavenly cause." You dreamed the impossible dream.

Peter's hero was Jesus. And Peter wanted to be a hero too.

Everybody was on edge. The Passover meal had been somber, with a certain heaviness between Jesus and Judas. There was talk about an impending arrest and death. Fear was in the air.

But when Jesus suggested things would get too

tough for them, that they would all fall away, Peter objected.

"No way, Lord. Not me. I don't care if they all run like scared rabbits. I'll stick it out. Those candy temple guards will have their hands full with me! You'll see!"

Peter could be very brave while in Jesus' presence.

When Jesus said not only that the disciples in general would fall away, but that Peter, in particular, would deny him three times, Peter looked hurt.

"Even if I have to die with you," Peter said, his voice cracking with emotion, "I'll never disown you."

It was a heroic moment for Peter. He loved Jesus. He had every intention of fighting for and dying with Jesus if that's what it took—and he said so. Whatever else we can say about him, Peter wanted to be a hero.

Following Jesus is about crying out for salvation, about a personal confession of faith, but it is also about becoming a hero. Christians, like Peter, are ordinary people following Jesus. Sometimes the path of discipleship passes through opportunities to turn the ordinary into the heroic—or into magnificent failure.

Jesus was arrested and the disciples fled, Matthew tells us, while Peter followed him *at a distance,* right up to the courtyard of the high priest to see the outcome of the trial before the Sanhedrin.

At a distance. Peter didn't run away and hide—
we have to give him credit for that. But neither did
he dare follow too closely. Within moments Peter
found that following Jesus at a distance left him vulnerable and afraid. Three times he had the chance
to boldly identify himself with his Lord and Master,
and thereby make good on his heroic promise to
Jesus, but each time he swung and missed. With an
oath to make his point, Peter struck out by denying
he even knew the man.

Peter could be heroic while standing at Jesus'
side, but found only failure when following him at a
distance.

I point no fingers at Peter. My own denials are a
dime a dozen. Why was I so embarrassed by the barber's question? Maybe because something about following Jesus sounds a little crazy sometimes. To
believe at all seems quaint and irrelevant to the
world I live in—let alone to make it a career. Maybe
I fear feeling foolish. Maybe I fear ridicule. Maybe
Peter did too.

What I love, though, is that we even have this
story at all. The only one who could have told it
was Peter himself. How many of us would allow
our greatest failure to be made public for future generations to read?

Salvation. Confession. Heroic commitment. Failure.
Peter was an ordinary man learning to follow Jesus.
In him we see ourselves. At times we find our hearts

brimming with joy and confidence as we walk closely with our Lord. In a triumphant moment we are capable of heroic decision and action on behalf of the one we serve and love. At other times we find ourselves confused and alone, unable to admit to even knowing him.

I find it encouraging to know Peter walked this road before me. I find it even more encouraging to remember that Jesus had a favorite nickname for his friend Peter; he called him "the Rock."

When Peter cried out in the overwhelming waves, Jesus grabbed him—an ordinary man—by the hand. When everyone was unsure, Jesus challenged him to speak up. When Peter wanted to be heroic, Jesus warned him of his weakness. When Peter failed, Jesus forgave him.

Like Peter, we cry for salvation when we're sinking.

We are capable of confessing the truth.

We sincerely want to be heroic.

We fail as often as we succeed.

Jesus will save us.

Jesus will challenge us.

Jesus will warn us.

Jesus will forgive us.

He might even give us each a new nickname.

CHAPTER EIGHT

A GOD WITH HAIR

*But before they came together, she was found
to be with child through the Holy Spirit. Because
Joseph her husband was a righteous man and did
not want to expose her to public disgrace, he had
in mind to divorce her quietly. But after he had
considered this, an angel of the Lord appeared to
him in a dream and said, "Joseph son of David, do
not be afraid to take Mary home as your wife,
because what is conceived in her is from the Holy
Spirit. She will give birth to a son, and you are to
give him the name Jesus, because he will save his
people from their sins."*

1:18-25

"Who is God?"

The words fairly shouted at me from the magazine rack at the checkout.

Right there next to "Man Gives Birth," and "Grandma Marries Alien" tabloid headlines, *Life* magazine framed the timeless query in bold white letters against a backdrop of a starry photo of the Milky Way.

The special issue chronicled how people, from a Filipino taxi driver to an Oxford dean, have sought to answer the question of God.

It's a good question. I have a hunch most of us ask it far more often than we admit—maybe even to ourselves.

Does God punish us with suffering?

Does God hear us when we pray?

Is God vengeful or pacifistic?

Does God speak to us? In dreams? In holy books? Through other people? How can we know?

Is God involved with the mundane things of everyday human life?

Will God help the Bears beat the Packers this weekend if I pray hard enough?

Most of the comments offered in the article expressed somewhat more spectacular images of

God than the one found in the first chapter of Matthew's Gospel:

Burmese monks praying before a huge gilded boulder perched on the edge of a cliff.

Japanese Buddhists praying under a cascading waterfall.

A Hindu worshiper kissing the feet of the colossal stone idol Jain.

Some were more ordinary.

A farmer in Florida said, "You can see God in a butter-bean patch."

My guess is most would be rather unimpressed with the scant eight verses Matthew devotes to the advent of God.

Indeed, if the eternal Creator God were to make an earthly appearance, one would expect a little more smoke and lightning to surround the event. It would seem more appropriate for the historic record to be detailed in a multivolume masterpiece or a television miniseries. But what we get is a few lines about a very ordinary birth. Ordinary, that is, except for the part about the virgin.

Two years ago I witnessed the birth of my first child, a son. Although he was eventually delivered by cesarean section, my wife first went through normal labor for about twelve hours. At one point, while I was in my Lamaze coaching position at Lorene's side, the doctor said he could see the baby and invited me to his vantage point. As I peered into the funnel-like instrument he held, sure enough, I could see my baby's dark hair. Excitement. Pride. Panic. Joy. I felt them all at that first glimpse of my child's hair, matted as it was with blood and amniotic fluid.

As I recall my son's red and swollen little face, the back of his head pushed all out of shape, I have to wonder why God would choose such a messy, ignoble, and ordinary way to enter our world. One has to assume, given his resources, that God could have staged his appearance in a million other, more magnificent ways.

He could have come as a caped superhero, able to render us awestricken by fantastic feats of physical or intellectual skill.

He could have turned the evening sky into a giant video screen and spoken to us in no uncertain terms.

But he didn't.

He came as a human baby—helpless, face swollen, hair matted on a tiny head pushed out of shape. Why?

A God with hair.

Just maybe God knew that if human beings need anything, it is a God with hair. We need, not the Dali Lama, high, hidden, and forbidding, but God in a baby's cry. A God of skin and breath and hair, who is known as well in the humility of a dirty diaper on Monday afternoon as in the magnificence of a cathedral on Sunday morning.

Sure, he is the Creator, God of the universe.

Sure, he is awesome and powerful.

Sure, he could crush us as if we were ants in an aquarium.

But just maybe he knew that before we needed his power we needed his love. Just maybe we need a God who identifies with us as much in the frying pan of suffering as on the mountaintop of joy, a God who remembers and speaks our name as much in our failure and ordinariness as in our triumphs.

We all carry some image of God in the portfolio of our imagination.

Is the God of our life angry and authoritarian—pointing a long accusatory finger like a mean elementary school principal? Is our God distant and vague, without a face, without a voice?

Look again at the God born in a barn.

Who is God? It is a haunting question to which, if we are honest, definitive answers are hard to come by. But for all we cannot say, we can say, if we take the gospel accounts seriously, that the God of the Bible is the God of ordinary people like you and me. He came as one of us, died for love of us, and lives again to come to us in our ordinary daily lives. For if God would go to such ridiculous and scandalous lengths to make himself present to the world—he will stop at nothing to come to you.

Look for him—but not only in the spectacular.

Listen for him—but not only in the thunder.

Look for his face and listen for his voice in the ordinary. There you will find him.

For there this God came to find you.

CHAPTER NINE

IS THIS THE ONE?

*When John heard in prison what Christ
was doing, he sent his disciples to ask him,
"Are you the one who was to come,
or should we expect someone else?"*

11:2

*Coming to his hometown, he began teaching the
people in their synagogue, and they were amazed.
"Where did this man get this wisdom and these
miraculous powers?" they asked. "Isn't this the
carpenter's son? Isn't his mother's name Mary, and
aren't his brothers James, Joseph, Simon and
Judas? Aren't all his sisters with us? Where then did
this man get all these things?" And they
took offense at him.*

13:54-57

He was right there in front of her eyes day after day. In the office. On assignment. At his typewriter. But Lois Lane could never let herself see Clark Kent as Superman. He just wasn't . . . well, SUPER enough.

His friends in the old stomping grounds of Nazareth had the same trouble with Jesus.

John, who pulled Jesus from the muddy Jordan waters with scraggly hair plastered against his forehead, saw the reflection of the Holy in his eyes as they first opened. But this same John, when his expectations weren't quite met in Jesus and his ministry, later asks, "Are you the one?"

In Nazareth the questions were probably less kind.

"Where does he get off sounding so high and mighty?"

"My word, I remember when he was just another runny-nosed little Nazarene boy—now he wants to preach to us?"

"If you ask me, he thinks he's too good for us."

Simply put, Jesus was not what the hometown crowd expected in the way of a Messiah. He was too . . . well, ordinary.

John was about to have his head served on a plat-

ter for denouncing the king's fling with his brother's
wife. And here is Jesus, the one he identified as the
Lamb of God who, in addition to healing the sick,
finds the time to reach out to prostitutes and con
men. Understandably perhaps, John had been looking for someone more apocalyptic—someone to put
on some dramatic spectacle to show he was the Messiah the Old Testament prophets wrote about.

Nazareth was a tough town. A blue-collar town
where you told it like it was, even if it wasn't pretty.

"So what if Mary and Joseph had gotten in
trouble? Sure they caught it pretty good for the one
about Jesus being from God and all, but hey, they
got on with their lives and people got off their
backs."

Until now.

"You just don't go into a town like Nazareth and
claim to be somebody you're not. We're all for finding a Messiah—this place could use some cleaning
up, especially the Romans—but, come on, he's got
to act a bit more like the king he claims to be."

"Yeah, get him talking about killing Romans, and
you'll see some excitement. That's the kingdom
we're interested in—not this forgiveness and righteousness mush."

We have a similar problem today. In a society that
worships only superstars, it almost goes without saying, we tend to want our Jesus to be more in the
Superman mold. If we are going to follow him, we
want more than his commitment to love us and a

command to love one another. We want some dramatic demonstrations of divine power, like melting all the world's tanks into tractors and combines to help feed the hungry. Or how about repairing the ozone layer overnight? And we'd like a miracle or two thrown in for ourselves. Like maybe having that stock we invested in double its value. Or trimming forty pounds off our paunchy flanks and reducing our cholesterol level by half—without so much as setting foot on a treadmill. Give us a square-jawed, no-nonsense, can-do Schwarzkopfian leader who turns up on the major networks, publishes a motivating autobiography (as if we don't already have enough), and has an *S* marked clearly on his chest and, oh yes, we will follow.

But if it were so, we may have a superhero, but we would not have a Savior. For although we may admire, applaud, fear, even worship our superheroes, we rarely love them and are even more rarely loved by them. And make no mistake, it is love that transforms people, not hero worship. The world would do far better to focus on righteousness over celebrity as the standard by which success is measured.

In Jesus, thanks be to God, we have both his personal love that forgives and accepts and his righteousness that sets an example we can follow. Not a superstar divinity who will grant an autograph or audience for a handsome fee, but rather a one-on-one God willing to hobnob with ordinary folks like you and me. Not a God concerned about his public image, but rather his private relationships.

Yes, Jesus is the one. Plain old Jesus. Just a carpenter from Nazareth. Does it all really make any difference?

Just ask Matthew, a dishonest businessman turned saint.

Try Mary Magdalene, from a demon-possessed woman to a devoted follower.

Or Zaccheus, despised con man who hosted Jesus at his own table.

Or Peter, spectacular failure turned pillar of strength.

I have an idea that Jesus, the five-star general, might ignore such problem cases as these, shunning them for the important task of drawing up battle strategies. But Jesus the Savior doesn't.

He had time. He loved, forgave, challenged, and transformed them all.

To the Jesus Matthew came to know, nothing was more important than time spent with ordinary people. It means you don't have to be somebody important—have a *Rev.* or *Dr.* in front of your name, or know someone who does—for Jesus to have time for you. It means he'll turn up in your ordinary life when you least expect it.

To listen to you.

To laugh or cry with you.

To forgive you.

To love you and give you hope.

He may not come in an *S* on his chest.

He may not come in lightning and thunder.
But he comes for you—and for me.
A superhero I can take or leave. But a friend like
that I'll take every time. How about you?

CHAPTER TEN

THE HUNGRY GOD

*Then Jesus was led by the Spirit into the desert
to be tempted by the devil. After fasting forty days
and forty nights, he was hungry. The tempter came
to him and said, "If you are the Son of God, tell
these stones to become bread."*

4:1-3

Have you ever been tempted to show off by jumping seventeen parked dune buggies on a motorcycle?

Have you lain awake at night dreaming of squeezing into black leotards and walking a tightrope strung between the World Trade Center towers?

Have you seriously considered how you might become king of the known world?

Neither have I.

Therefore I find it difficult to relate to the second and third carrots a wily Satan dangles before Jesus in the desert. But, oh, that first one!

Satan's second and third temptations are rather dramatic and spectacular in scope. The second challenge was for Jesus to throw himself off the pinnacle of the temple, trusting angels to catch him before splattering on the sidewalk. The third is a mountaintop offer to rule the world in exchange for Jesus worshiping him just once. But the first is so ordinary that one almost doesn't notice it just might be the most diabolical.

Bread. Satan begins his seduction of the Son of God with ordinary bread. Not money. Not an alluring woman. Bread.

Jesus was hungry. He had prepared for this con-

frontation with his old rival by fasting and praying,
Matthew writes, for forty days. In doing so Jesus,
the incarnation of the living God, became hungry.

I have never fasted forty days, nor, I suspect, have
you. But I have managed, on several occasions, to
avoid going to the refrigerator (although I usually
have to be in another state to do so) just long
enough to feel the first pangs of what might be hunger. It's sad, but after several hours I find myself
fantasizing about what I'm going to eat next time I
have the chance—and how much. I can only imagine how Jesus' body must have craved nourish-
ment—a piece of fruit, a bowl of soup, a hunk of
bread, a couple of sticks of celery, anything!

Satan, not being one to miss an opportunity,
chooses this moment to issue his first and greatest
temptation. "If you are the Son of God," he hisses,
"turn these stones into bread." Bread, of all things.
Such an ordinary and innocent thing. Just a word,
and he could be savoring a warm loaf of Jewish rye.

Why not?

It's only bread, after all.

And you're only human.

Just this once.

So it is that Satan lived up to his reputation by
tempting a hungry man with bread. But not only
that. He tempted Jesus to abuse his relationship
with the Father for a selfish need. Behind this temptation lay another—to listen to the voice hissing
from the darkness and do its bidding. And Satan

used such ordinary things to weave his web. Bread
and hunger.

Scripture tells us Jesus was "led by the Spirit into
the desert to be tempted by the devil." For some reason I had always assumed Satan was the one who
led Jesus to the wilderness—in order to attack when
Jesus was weak and alone. I'm now convinced the
Spirit led Jesus to the desert to prepare him, to
make him strong. The desert, for Jesus, seems to
have been a favorite place of withdrawal for communion with the Father. Throughout the Gospels
we notice him doing just that before or during times
of stress or decision.

When he needed to gather trusted friends around
him to begin his public ministry, "he went out into
the mountains to pray, and prayed all night. At day-
break he called together his followers and chose
twelve of them" (Luke 6:12).

When the specter of the Cross loomed on his hori-
zon, "he went on a little further and fell to the
ground and prayed" (Mark 14:35).

When he faced a day full of crowds pressing near
to get a piece of him, "he was up long before day-
break and went out alone into the wilderness to
pray" (Mark 1:35).

We learn two things from this Faustian confrontation.

Make that three.

Although Satan is perhaps best known for seducing

us with the lovely, his tactics seem also to include
the ordinary and seemingly innocent.

Jesus knew the sound of Satan's voice.

Our triumph depends on our preparation.

When we think of temptation, we are likely to
wind up at either of two extremes. On the one
hand, we think of *temptation* as a word fossilized in
our theological dictionaries—a quaint but extinct
concept that went the way of the dinosaur, altar
call, and unpadded pews.

On the other hand, we think 42nd Street—triple-
X movie parlors, drug pushers littering the street
corners, hookers strutting their stuff, leaving little to
the imagination. Temptation becomes the spectacu-
larly sinful, the sleaze and grotesquely exaggerated
carnality of our culture.

Interestingly, both extremes leave most of us off
the hook. Satan extends no such courtesy.

Check out his modus operandi.

A question and a piece of fruit in the garden.
"Did God really say that? Surely he created this lus-
cious, good-tasting fruit for your enjoyment. It's
even healthy for you."

A comely neighbor bathing within sight of a
bored king. You can almost hear the serpentine
voice. "You've paid your dues—a lifetime of danger
and victorious battles—time to kick back and enjoy
some of the fruits of your labor."

And then an offer of bread to a hungry man.

We live in a world that has elevated temptation to
an art form. Food, drink, cars, clothes, shoes, beer,

tobacco are hawked shamelessly by advertising campaigns that dangle the carrots of success, sex-appeal, and material comfort through our television screens. Despite much progress in women's rights, women's bodies are used to sell everything from V-6 engines to diet soft drinks to sports magazines—let alone the rows of titillating covers that adorn the racks of newsstands everywhere. Note well that, while not dramatic or disgusting, the voice of the tempter still can be heard.

"You can have it all."

"Just once."

"It won't hurt anybody,"

"You deserve a little pleasure."

Ordinary, everyday temptation. Hunger and bread. One can almost hear Satan laughing with delight.

"He was tempted in all things as we are, yet without sin," proclaims the writer to the Hebrews. Several years ago Martin Scorsese directed the film *The Last Temptation of Christ*, which was an adaptation of Greek writer Níkos Kazantzakís's novel of the same title. While the film drew little critical praise and an understandable backlash from the conservative Christian community, it provided much food for thought. Kazantzakís begins with Luke's version of Jesus' temptation in the desert, which concludes with the darkly suggestive line "and Satan left him until an opportune time."

According to the novel, the more "opportune" time occurred as Jesus hung on the cross. Just after

Jesus screams, "Why have you forsaken me," Satan
appears again. He comes in the form of a little girl
and simply tells Jesus that he has done enough, that
the Father is pleased, and that he can come down
from his cross. She walks him through what would
be the rest of his life. Marriage. Children. A home
and a tidy little carpentry business. Grandkids. In
the end, Jesus recognizes his old nemesis, resists,
and crawls back to the cross to die as the Savior.
Whatever else Kazantzakís and Scorsese may have
gotten wrong about Jesus, they got Satan right.

Jesus knew the tempter's voice in all its madden-
ing deception. Ordinary things, twisted around lies,
hidden behind questions. So easy to hear, so hard to
recognize, harder still to resist.

But Jesus did resist.

Here's how.

He prayed.

We are told he was led by the Spirit to fast and
pray for forty days. Notice he did so *before* the
temptation came.

There is a great secret here.

Prayer was Jesus' preparation, not his escape.

He did not wait until the aroma of fresh baked
loaves wafted by his nostrils. He did not wait until
he heard the slithering of the serpent's belly upon
the sand. He prayed in preparation. Did he pray asking for ears to recognize the soothing wickedness of
Satan's voice? Did he ask for eyes to see through the
devilish, but oh so attractive, smoke screens? Did he
ask the Father to so fill him with love, security, and

steadfast commitment that no nook or cranny of his heart would yet be empty and yearning, thus vulnerable? We don't know. But we do know that his triumph was in his preparation.

So is ours.

Ordinary prayer.

So often we see prayer as what we do when the heat is on. When the hammer of bad news threatens to shatter our glass lives; when the voice of the tempter beckons softly in an unclaimed corner of our hearts; when we feel ourselves caught in the undertow, then we think to toss up a prayer. These are emergency prayers. Desperate. Spectacular in intensity and earnestness. But they do not prepare. They rescue.

Jesus did not wait for the emergency. He prepared. Ordinary, everyday, daily prayer. Prayer not only for answers. Not only for the spectacular miracle. Not only in tragedy or temptation. Not prayer as a shopping list of requests, nor a set of distasteful circumstances to be avoided, nor bone-rattling potholes in our pathway to be negated or otherwise smoothed over, but prayer as preparation. Prayer that is more listening than speaking, seeking more internal changes than the manipulation of external events. Prayer for discipline, strength, and perseverance more than for good days, easy paths, and ready-made successes. Prayer as communion with the one who teaches our ears to recognize the voice, our eyes to see though the lies, and our hearts to be filled beyond all need.

Yes, the first one was the hardest. Hunger and bread. Jesus was hungry, terribly so, as are you and I. But he resisted the temptation to deny his relationship with the Father for a quick fix. He confronted the smooth and coaxing voice of the tempter. But he did not do so easily.

He prepared forty days for the moment he would say no.

Do we prepare as diligently for our daily confrontation with the tempter?

Do we recognize his voice in the cacophony of our lives?

We do well to remember that Satan does not start with the big ones—drugs, adultery, murder—but with ordinary things like fun, lust, greed, hunger, and bread.

Our triumph depends upon our preparation.

The power of ordinary prayer.

CHAPTER ELEVEN

WHY?

From the sixth hour until the ninth hour
darkness came over all the land. About the ninth
hour Jesus cried out in a loud voice, "Eloi, Eloi,
lama sabachthani,"—*which means, "My God,*
my God, why have you forsaken me?"

27:45-46

"*Eloi, Eloi, lama sabachthani?*"

Did the words explode in a guttural cry that split the darkening sky like a thunderbolt? Did they spill softly from swollen lips so that even those close by had to ask, "What did he say?"

"*Eloi, Eloi, lama sabachthani?*"—which means, "My God, my God, why have you forsaken me?"

Whether shouted or whispered, the words hang there in chapter 27 of Matthew, stark, full of pain, and unanswerable.

It is at this point in our observance of Christ's Passion, the events surrounding his death and resurrection, that we want to fast-forward to the happy ending. We can stand at the foot of the cross and watch, eyes moist with admiration and love, as our Lord forgives those who drove the nails into his hands and feet, whose spit dried on his face. We can meditate on his pardon of the thief and the promise of paradise. We can even bear to see the spear thrust into his side and see the blood and water flow mingled down—the symbol of our salvation. But when Jesus heaves this question heavenward, everything in us wants to turn away.

"My God, my God, why have you forsaken me?"

We want to run from the question on the cross in

all its ugliness to the beauty and joy of the empty tomb. Perhaps we want to run because we never want to ask the question ourselves. Maybe we run because we already have.

I know I have.

I suspect, when we are honest, we admit that we have asked God why he abandoned us at a time we could have used a little divine intervention. Maybe we didn't scream and shake our fist at the night sky. Or maybe we did. Either way, the question was there, lurking about the shadows of our heart. "Why God? Why?"

The question stabbed my broken heart and sledge-hammered my fragile faith as I stared through tears at the casket carrying my youngest brother. "Why God? Where were you on that godforsaken road outside Charlotte, North Carolina, when John's motorcycle inexplicably crossed the center line into the path of an oncoming truck? Why us?"

What has caused your *why?*

The death of a loved one?

Divorce?

Broken relationship with a child?

Loss of a job? a home?

Cancer? Depression? Psychiatric illness? Pain?

To be human is to ask why.

To be a person of faith is to ask, "Why, God?"

Someone has said that from our human perspective God is often more conspicuous in his absence than in his presence. This so often seems to be true.

Stop. Turn around. Let's not run from the cross and the one who puts voice to the question of our heart. Walk with me back up the infamous hillside and look again at the one we call Jesus.

What drove him to utter the wrenching words? Why did Jesus ask *why?*

Was it the pain that tore at his flesh?

Was it the spiritual loneliness as the Father turned his back on the sin of the world?

Was it disappointment? Had he, as some would say, expected a miraculous last-minute reprieve?

Was it the abandonment of the very friends in whom he had invested his life?

Did he feel anger? Resentment? Sadness?

We don't know. We can't know. But I do know I'm terribly glad Jesus put voice to his despair. The longer I kneel at the foot of his cross, the more I meditate on the one who knew such loneliness, such anguish, the less alone I feel in mine.

Sooner or later the *why* question rears its unwelcome head. Whether we ask it for ourselves or on behalf of someone we love, the time will come. For me it came sooner. Perhaps it has for you too.

We wonder if God is who we always believed him to be. If he is not, then we wonder what beliefs, what images we can conjure up to adequately understand our experience. We wonder if our prayers really make any difference. We wonder if our faith can bear such questioning.

"My God. My God. Why have you forsaken me?"

I do not know the answer to the question. I do

not believe that God forsakes. I do know it sometimes feels that way.

So did Jesus.

If you are asking, or have ever asked, "Why,
God?" go back to Golgotha. When you find yourself wondering where the power of God is when life
becomes a tangle of twisted metal, go back to Cal-
vary.

There you will see power abdicated on behalf of
love.

There you will see you are not abandoned.

There you will see one who stretched out his
arms wide enough to embrace our pain in all its
ambiguity.

If there is an answer to your particular question,
he will provide it. If, upon plumbing the depths of
human hope, scaling the heights of divine wisdom,
no answer can be found to soothe your pain, then
look again at the one on the tree.

On his face you will find your own tears glisten-
ing. In his arms you will find fierce comfort. And
when there is no answer but to endure, he will be
sufficient.

He is Jesus, whose love is unbounded by suffering, who is unafraid of our fears and doubt, una-
shamed to call us friends—a man of sorrows,
acquainted with grief.

He is Jesus—my Lord and my God.

CHAPTER TWELVE

THE GOD WHO TOUCHED

A man with leprosy came and knelt before him and said, "Lord, if you are willing, you can make me clean." Jesus reached out his hand and touched the man. "I am willing," he said. "Be clean!"

8:2-3

At first he thought nothing of it. A dry patch of skin near his hairline on the right side of his forehead. He resolved to stop using the soap his wife used. That stuff would dry out anybody's skin.

But different soap didn't help. In fact the whitish spot now included an angry red ring. *Must be infected,* he thought, and smeared a dab of healing ointment on it every morning.

Within a few weeks he found himself smoothing his hair so as to cover the spot as much as possible. He bought a larger hat in the marketplace and joked with his wife about looking more like a shepherd now.

He was hoeing his garden without his tunic when a friend commented on the dry skin on the back of his elbow. "Hey Jeremiah, you oughta try some of this olive oil—I use it all the time—it'll clear that stuff up in no time."

Three other kinds of lotion didn't work either.

The second spot began to turn red, and the first ulcerated and began to ooze fluid. At first his wife wanted him to see a physician. But that was before the second spot. He could tell now she was more than concerned. She was afraid.

He didn't tell her what happened while he was

working with their son the other day . . . the strange
tingling numbness he felt in his fingers. He had
dropped the trowel a couple of times, not by mistake, but because he couldn't *feel* it in his fingers.

He was more than afraid. He knew.

Finally, one night as they lay together in the darkness, he broke the silence.

"Honey, I, uh, I think I should go to the priest."
He tried to sound matter-of-fact, but his voice gave
away his fear.

"I know," she said after a time. Her voice
sounded so small.

"It's probably nothing . . . he's seen a million
cases like this . . . he'll know what to do."

She didn't say anything. But he could hear her
sniffing back tears and swallowing hard. Then she
put her head against his chest and hugged him hard.

It would be the last time she touched him.

The waiting area outside the priest's chambers was
full of people. The place smelled foul, and it would
be a long wait. He tried to recite parts of the Torah,
but his mind kept wandering, and his eye kept
going back to the man sitting across the room. He
had to assume it was a man from the clothes he
wore. He couldn't tell from the face. The nose was
mostly gone, and the face was covered with ulcerated sores. The hand, he could see, was gnarled and
clawlike. He kept looking at the sores—they were
whitish-red—and running his fingers over the one
on his own forehead.

He waited two hours, but his actual time with the priest was no more than five minutes. The priest looked tired. He looked carefully at the sore and leaned close. Jeremiah could smell the priest's breath. He probed with something that looked like a small wooden spoon. It didn't hurt.

He had Jeremiah strip to his underclothing and lie face down on a small bed. With his wooden object he poked over the skin on Jeremiah's back— stopping several times to scrape lightly.

"Had any tingling or numbness in your hands or feet?"

Jeremiah thought about lying but said, "Maybe a little."

"Tell me when you feel pain."

Jeremiah could tell by his voice the priest was at his feet. "I feel some pressure."

"Any pain?"

"Uh . . . no."

"Get dressed and have a seat by my table there— we have to talk."

The priest sat down heavily in his swivel chair. He rubbed his eyes with the thumb and forefinger of one hand.

"Jeremiah," he started while putting his glasses back on, "I'm afraid I have bad news. You have leprosy."

The word stung as if he'd been slapped in the face. *Leprosy.*

Of course he'd suspected it when he had to start hiding the first sore. He had pushed the word from his mind when he was working without his tunic on and his friend had noticed the second sore. But now the news exploded like shrapnel across the face of his life.

"It's too early to tell what type you have—how long you can expect to . . . You might have a less severe variety. But you do have it. . . . I'm sorry, Jeremiah . . . you know the rules."

Jeremiah wanted to look up, but found himself unable to raise his head.

"By sundown tonight," the priest went on from memory, "you must be outside the city limits. Once you're checked into the colony, your family can visit once a month in the visiting zone. Whenever in hearing distance of the general population, you must shout, 'Unclean, unclean.' If you fail to do so, or come within twenty paces of a clean person, he will have the right to stone you to death."

It was nine years ago. He could still hear the words as if spoken yesterday. But it felt like a lifetime ago or more.

He thought maybe the monthly visits were the worst. His life had ended with the pronouncement of "unclean!" He lived as a dead man among other dead men. Wretched excuses of untouchable humanity. But when he saw his wife and son standing twenty paces away, tears in their eyes, he was reminded that part of him still lived. The only part that yet could feel pain—his heart—and it was breaking again. The visits were what he lived for, but they were the worst.

When he first heard the rumor, he dismissed it without a second thought. His hopes had been raised and then dashed too many times for him to give serious attention to a healing prophet from Nazareth.

But when, during a visit, his wife said she'd actually seen Jesus in person . . . that he'd healed all kinds of people . . . that crowds followed him everywhere, then he allowed himself to hope.

"But I'm a leper. The law won't let him get close to me."

"But he can heal by just speaking. If he could just see you . . ."

To go home again. To hold his wife close. To wrestle with his boy—now a strapping teenager. He hated himself for hoping. He hated himself for not hoping.

He decided. Even if it meant death by stoning, he would find this prophet Jesus. Even if it meant groveling like a fool in the dust, he would do it.

His friends in the colony tried to dissuade him.

"Jeremiah," they cautioned, "we don't want to see you hurt."

"I can't hurt anymore."

"But you're a leper!"

"I know what I am. I'm a husband and a father."

"Jeremiah, look at yourself," one of them said, holding up a shard of glass. "You're not like you were when you got here."

It was true, of course. Most of his hair had fallen out, his skin was leathery and blistered. He grabbed the mirror and threw it with all his might against the rocky cliff wall.

"But they'll stone you."

"Yeah, maybe they will."

"Unclean! Unclean!"

"Leper!" taunted the teenage boy who could have been his son's playmate.

"There's no place for you here," the mother shrieked angrily over her shoulder as she took her children off the street.

"Go back to the colony," growled an old man as he picked up a stone the size of a fist.

"Unclean! Unclean!" He walked as fast as he dared toward the center of the crowd. Startled people heard his cry and peeled out of his path in panic.

"Leper!"

"Get him out of here!"

"Unclean! Unclean!" He charged ahead waiting for the first blow to fall.

Suddenly he found himself at the center of the mob. The taunts and threats grew silent. The only other figure in the clearing turned as if Jeremiah had spoken his name. He hadn't yet said a word. Their eyes met, but Jeremiah quickly lowered his head and fell to his knees.

"Lord, . . ." he'd practiced his speech a thousand times on the walk, but now he could only manage a simple sentence. "If you are willing, you can make me clean."

His head was buried in his chest. His arms folded around himself tightly as if to keep his pain from spilling all over the ground. He felt himself heave with one great sob.

And then Jesus touched him.

With hands clamped to the sides of his face, Jesus guided him to his feet. Then he lifted his face.

It was the first time he'd been touched by another human being in more than nine years.

"I am willing," Jesus said in a firm, clear voice, hands pressed against Jeremiah's cratered face. "Be clean!"

Jesus touched him.

When the world declared him to be untouchable, when even friends rejected him as unclean, dirty, infectious.

Jesus touched him.

When he most despised and hated himself, when he refused to look at his own vileness for fear of retching.

Jesus touched him.

In placing his hands on the decaying flesh of the leper, Jesus shattered a petrified religious code that could exclude but not heal. He put to death the image of a God more concerned with external cleanliness than inner pain.

We are the leper.

No, we don't go around shouting, "Unclean! Unclean!" Not in so many words. But we are leprous nonetheless. We carry with us the festered scars of rejection and loss. We hide so much of ourselves away from view—unacceptable, unpresentable, full of shame. We allow no one to come near enough to those places to touch.

And no one tries.

Do you have such an untouchable place? An unclean place? Perhaps you are one of the legion of sexual abuse survivors. Your secret is so dark and shameful you hid from even yourself for so long. Now you feel ugly, unpresentable, unlovable.

Maybe you have been on the other side of that pain. An abuser. You are unclean, unable to purge the guilt from your soul.

Maybe your leprosy is not so dramatic. You simply haven't been deemed "beautiful" by the standards of our world. Fun, friends, romance always seem to be happening behind the warm glow of light in someone else's window. You are left outside looking in, shivering and alone.

Jesus wants to touch you.

Not just with a superficial pat on the back, or a feel-good hug. He wants to touch you at the place you are most untouchable. He doesn't put on a mask and rubber gloves, he doesn't recoil in disgust. He takes you in his strong hands and says, "I am willing. Be clean!"

To receive such a transforming and healing touch, we must get up from our place of despair and shame, ignore the voices that ridicule and tell us it's no use, step with boldness out into the light of his presence, and fall in confession and hope at his feet.

He is willing, and we will be clean.

CHAPTER THIRTEEN

SPAGHETTI JESUS

*"When the Son of Man comes in his glory,
and all the angels with him, he will sit on his
throne in heavenly glory. All the nations will be
gathered before him, and he will separate the
people one from another as a shepherd separates
the sheep from the goats. He will put the sheep
on his right and the goats on his left.
"Then the King will say to those on his right,
'Come, you who are blessed by my Father; take
your inheritance, the kingdom prepared since the
creation of the world. For I was hungry and you
gave me something to eat, I was thirsty and you
gave me something to drink, I was a stranger and
you invited me in, I needed clothes and you clothed
me, I was sick and you looked after me, I was
in prison and you came to visit me.'
"Then the righteous will answer him, 'Lord,
when did we see you hungry and feed you, or
thirsty and give you something to drink? When did
we see you a stranger and invite you in, or needing
clothes and clothe you? When did we see you
sick or in prison and go to visit you?'
"The King will reply, 'I tell you the truth, whatever
you did for one of the least of these brothers of
mine, you did for me.'"*

25:31-40

Jesus in spaghetti sauce. That's what motorists said they saw on a billboard in DeKalb, Georgia.

I've seen the huge statue of *El Cristo* with arms outstretched in Santa Cruz, Bolivia. I've seen the *Touchdown Jesus* mural on the campus of Notre Dame University. I've even seen little magnetized plastic Jesuses for the dashboard of your car. But I've never seen Jesus in spaghetti sauce.

But Joyce Simpson did.

She happened to look up as she drove out of the Texaco gas station and there he was, deep-set eyes, beard, crown of thorns, and all, staring back at her from an ad for Pizza Hut. The ad featured a fork full of spaghetti and copy that read, "Spaghetti Junction." If you know where to look, right above the dot of the *i* in *spaghetti,* enmeshed in a drooping heap of pasta and meat sauce, you just might see something that looks like Jesus.

The spaghetti Jesus.

He was sitting hunched against the dark and cold on a street corner in La Paz, Bolivia. He couldn't have been more than eight or nine years old. He was crying.

My brother and I were leading a team of Christian college athletes on a tour of Bolivia. We traveled the length and breadth of the country, playing games, giving clinics, and speaking to groups of coaches, young athletes, and thousands of spectators not only about basketball, but about our faith as well. Huffing and puffing in the 13,000-foot altitude, we had played the La Paz city champions this particular night in the beautiful downtown sports arena, then had dinner in a nice restaurant. Even though it was quite chilly at night in that thin air, we decided to walk back to our hotel. It was about 11:00 P.M. when we saw him—sitting right at the corner where we had to turn.

Bolivia is the second poorest country in the western hemisphere—just behind Haiti. A country of stunning physical beauty, with towering snowcapped mountain ranges, tropical forests, and sweeping high deserts, Bolivia is also a place of equally stunning poverty and suffering.

The economy is in shambles. When we left in December 1985, we were getting 1.7 million Bolivian pesos for a dollar. Professionals might earn the equivalent of thirty-five dollars a month—if they were fortunate enough to have a job. The rate of infant mortality was many times higher than in the U.S. Nearly a quarter of a million children died each year from diarrhea and its complications—the victims of malnutrition, unsanitary conditions, and nonpotable water.

Why he was crying I don't know. I almost didn't see him in the darkness. But there he was, dressed in raggedy clothes—no overcoat, just a tattered sweater—crying into the night.

Was he cold?

Was he hungry?

Where was his family? Did he have a family? Was he lonely?

Who was he?

We didn't find the answers to these questions because we walked back to our hotel. We had seen the little boy. We had heard his cry. But we didn't speak Spanish very well. We didn't know what we could do. We didn't know who he was or where he belonged. So we walked the rest of the way in silence.

In the silence I can hear him crying still.

At least twice in Matthew's Gospel, Jesus makes rather alarming statements about where we might look if we desire to see him.

The disciples ask Jesus to resolve their debate about who would be the greatest in the kingdom. They seemed to assume it would be one of them. They wound up with egg on their faces as Jesus said, in effect, "You're looking in the wrong place—you're not even in the right ballpark."

> *"I tell you the truth, unless you change and become like little children, you will never enter the kingdom of heaven. Therefore, whoever humbles himself like this child is the greatest in the kingdom of heaven. And whoever*

*welcomes a little child like this in my name
welcomes me."* 18:3-5

Something about children seems to draw us very
near to the heart of Jesus. Something about inno-
cence. Something about beauty. Something about
an unspeakable tenderness and love. And something in me remembers a little boy on the side of
the road.

A few chapters later, Jesus spins a metaphor of
sheep, goats, and final judgment. It's enough to
make the "wool" on the back of your neck stand on
end. The sheep will be separated from the goats, he
says, not by the bony little horns, but by whether or
not they fed him when he was hungry, gave him a
drink when he was thirsty, gave him a bed and
home when he was homeless, clothed him when he
was naked, and visited him in prison.

"But Lord," they ask understandably, "when did
we see *you* hungry or thirsty, or homeless, or naked,
or in prison?

"When did we see you?"

*"I tell you the truth, whatever you did for one
of the least of these brothers of mine, you did
for me."* 25:40

Could it be that in some unfathomable way Jesus
can be known in the tear-streaked faces and ravaged
bodies of the world's forgotten and despised?

We want to see Jesus. We don't have the advantage the disciples had of hanging out with him every day in the Galilean countryside. We believe he came in the flesh as the incarnate God, but we can't see him, touch him, watch him eat fish, or laugh at a good joke.

Trouble is, Jesus keeps showing up where we least expect to find him.

He always has.

In a Bethlehem stable.

In a tax collector's home.

Touching a leper.

Healing on the sabbath.

Forgiving and befriending a prostitute.

With children.

Hungry in the desert.

Naked and thirsty on the cross.

In the lonely cry of a Bolivian boy.

"Lord, when did we see you?"

I doubt that Jesus is in that billboard advertising Pizza Hut spaghetti. People who see such things may be more than a few notches off center. And it probably is a wobbly illustration for what Jesus is trying to teach us. But something about being able to see Jesus, something about looking for him in unexpected places, gets my attention. It reminds me of how often I may miss opportunities to meet my Savior face-to-face because I am not looking for him.

I know now it was Jesus I heard in the little boy's

cry. Jesus was in the child's tears. Only I didn't see him then. I walked right on by.

To see Jesus you have to know where to look. And you have to learn how to see.

Open our eyes, Lord, that we might see.

CHAPTER FOURTEEN

CHRIST THE QUESTION

*As Jesus and his disciples were leaving Jericho,
a large crowd followed him. Two blind men were
sitting by the roadside, and when they heard that
Jesus was going by, they shouted, "Lord,
Son of David, have mercy on us!"
The crowd rebuked them and told them to be
quiet, but they shouted all the louder, "Lord,
Son of David, have mercy on us!"
Jesus stopped and called them. "What do you
want me to do for you?" he asked.
"Lord," they answered, "we want our sight." Jesus
had compassion on them and touched their eyes.
Immediately they received their sight
and followed him.*

20:29-34

It was the first day of a new semester at the midwestern Christian university I was attending. The class was Theoretical Foundations for Christian Education. A tall, rather intense-looking man with glasses and a short beard stood at the blackboard. His reputation as a fine, if somewhat controversial, professor preceded him. The students, most preparing for some kind of Christian ministry, waited anxiously for Dr. Taylor's first lecture. He picked up a piece of chalk and turned without a word to write on the board. Fresh-faced Christian ed majors arranged in rows behind him strained forward to see what he had written.

Would it be a Scripture reference they could look up in the study Bibles placed prominently on top of their stacks of books and notebooks?

Would it be a reading assignment for the following day? Or maybe just his office hours?

What they saw as he stepped aside caused something between a "Huh?" and a gasp to rise spontaneously from the class.

"CHRIST IS NOT THE ANSWER."

Not exactly what they expected to see. After all, they, or their parents, were paying good money to learn the answers, Christian answers, biblical

answers, to life's problems. More than a few had
"Jesus is the answer" bumper stickers on their cars.
They were in the class to learn all the answers Jesus
has to give—and how to share them with the world.

The professor stood for a long time next to the
disturbing message on the blackboard. Some students squirmed in their chairs, sending a chorus of
squeaks bouncing off the acoustically tiled ceiling.
Some dutifully recorded "Christ is not the answer"
on a clean, white page in their spiral notebooks.
Some just stared with a wide-eyed, deer-caught-in-
the-headlights kind of look. Then the professor
wrote a second line under the first.

"CHRIST IS ALWAYS THE QUESTION."

Two beggars sit in rags on the edge of a dusty road.
They sit and beg because they are blind. There is no
clinic, no braille training center, no cataract or laser
surgery to which they can appeal. They feel the peb-
bles tossed at them by prankster youths; they taste
the bread crusts given by compassionate passersby;
they smell the sweaty beasts who lap dirty water
from the side of the road; and they hear the chatter
of day. But their world is veiled in darkness.

They have heard, in bits and pieces of passing
conversation, news of one called Jesus. Amid the
scuffling of sandaled feet and the *plink* of coins in
their clay jars, they have heard things too wonderful
to believe.

"Whaddaya think about this new prophet from
Nazareth?"

A hundred pair of flopping feet make the response difficult to hear.

"You mean Jesus?"

"Yeah, they say he's a miracle worker."

"That's what they always say."

A donkey brays. Chickens cluck and peck at their feet, looking for crumbs.

"My cousin saw him last week—was in the front row—saw him touch a leper."

"He touched a *leper?*"

"Yup, and my cousin said the leper walked right by him afterward, and his skin was smooth as a baby's bum."

Someone yells, "Here, catch!"

The two blind men hear coins bouncing in the dirt around them. A group of laughing people leave them groveling after shekels they cannot see.

"Nobody knows what to make of him. His teaching is drawing huge crowds. There are reports that with one touch he has healed all kinds of sick people—even the blind. They say he even claims to forgive sin."

"If you ask me, he's some kind of fraud. His type is dangerous."

"If you believe that, I've got a palace in Galilee I'd like to sell you."

Did they hear it right? Jesus had even healed the blind? With one touch? They both knew, of course, that it wasn't possible. But if it was . . .

They felt the crowd approaching through the trembling of the ground even before they heard the

general hubbub. What kind of thing was this? It
wasn't a feast day. By the sound of it, neither was it
a demonstration against the Romans. People were
walking slowly, quietly, yet excitement was in the
air. Then they heard the name.

"Jesus is coming. Jesus is coming."

Little boys and girls were dancing and repeating
the words over and over in a kind of singsong game.

"Jesus is coming, la, tee-dah, tee-dah!"

"Jesus!" The name flashed like lightning in their
brains. . . . *Jesus!* the one who had cleansed the
leper. *Jesus!* who had forgiven sin. *Jesus!* who had
healed even the blind with just one touch. They
could not let this moment pass.

"Lord!" they shouted into the milling crowd,
"Son of David!" It was the highest compliment they
could think of. "Have mercy on us!"

"Hey, knock it off! The man's trying to teach!"

"Pipe down—and get off the road—you're gonna
get hurt."

"Lord!" they shouted all the louder, ignoring the
shushing of the crowd. "Son of David, have mercy
on us!"

"Lord! Lord!" Could he hear them? "Have mercy
on us! Mercy! Mercy!" Would he heed their cries
with so many pressing about?

"Shut up you two—or we'll shut you up. We
came to hear Jesus—not two banty-roosters crow-
ing on the side of the road!"

The crowd around them grew suddenly still.

"Make room, make room. The Master's coming through."

"Shhh! . . . It's Jesus! Look!"

"What's he doing?"

They felt him looking at them before they heard his voice. They were ashamed and afraid. Their squawking had interrupted his teaching. Their hoarse yelping ceased. They knelt on all fours in the dirt and waited for his rebuke.

"What do you want me to do for you?" Jesus asked.

No rebuke, only a simple question. A question that called from them their deepest longing, that for which they were almost afraid to ask, that which they were all but sure could never happen.

"Lord, we want to see."

"What do you want me to do for you?"

Indeed! Either Jesus was asking a dumb question, he was flippantly insensitive to the blind men's situation, or he had other reasons for asking the obvious.

"What do you want me to do for you?"

Heal your body?

Encourage your heart?

Forgive your sins?

Call you to obedience?

Be your personal Santa Claus?

I have an idea Jesus used questions as more than just a creative teaching device.

"Who do you say that I am?" (16:15)

A quaint idea?
An ancient myth?
A great man and teacher?
King of kings?"
"Can you drink the cup I am going to drink?"
(20:22)
"Well, I'll take about half a cup."
"Thanks, but I'm not that thirsty."
"With your help, to the dregs."

My professor friend went on to say that before
Jesus is the answer, he is always the question. Questions always call us to confession, decision, and
response. We can hide from statements, but we are
laid bare by questions.

The Jesus we meet in Matthew's Gospel stands as
a great question mark on the pages of our lives.

Who do we say that he is?
What do we want him to do for us?
Are we able to drink from his cup?

> *Jesus had compassion on them and touched
> their eyes. Immediately they received their sight
> and followed him.*

Questions like this challenge us to have the courage to ask greatly, receive humbly, and follow boldly.

CHAPTER FIFTEEN

LIKE A TREASURE HIDDEN

The kingdom of heaven is like treasure hidden in a field. When a man found it, he hid it again, and then in his joy went and sold all he had and bought that field.

13:44

Listed as one of the one hundred most important Americans of the twentieth century by *Life* magazine, Wallace Hume Carothers had a gift for understanding chemistry. He invented the synthetic rubber now called neoprene. In 1935 he mixed coal, air, and water to produce a test-tube fiber that was used in everything from parachutes to sutures during World War II. Despite all this, the inventor of Polymer 66 poisoned himself at age forty-one before his miracle fabric received its more popular name, nylon. Why? He had become despondent over being a chemist instead of a singer.

"And I still haven't found what I'm looking for." A popular rock-and-roll band made famous this phrase from one of their hit songs a few years ago. It became a sort of anthem for a generation—a generation with a haunting sense that something is out there that will bring ultimate happiness. Perhaps it is a pot of gold at the end of a rainbow, a winning number for the state lottery, falling in love with the right person. For Carothers it was leaving the mundane world of chemistry behind for a glamorous career as a cabaret singer.

Most of us look into the fogged mirror every morning with only the slightest notion we are about to embark on a treasure hunt. Whether we could articulate our hunt in so many words is doubtful, but we are, no doubt, hunting for treasure.

We hunt for it in work, in paychecks, in success.

We hunt for it in leisure, in fitness centers, on vacations. We hunt for it in our relationships, in more exotic sexual experiences, in therapy.

We hunt for it in our children, in their achievements, in their need for us.

Wallace Carothers hunted for it in his misguided dreams.

The kingdom of heaven, says Jesus, is like a treasure. Hidden treasure. In two brief sentences that any second grader could understand, Jesus suggests four truths many Ph.D.s fail to grasp.

1. Life is a treasure hunt.
2. It helps to have a good map.
3. The price is high.
4. The end is joy.

We are the man in Jesus' parable, digging hole after hole in the field, hoping to hit pay dirt.

For better or worse, we are also following some map on our hunt. We get our maps from various places.

We may inherit them from our families. "It's a dog-eat-dog world out there, Son, and if you ain't the lead dog, the scenery don't change much."

We might absorb them from our culture. "Have it

your way!" "You can have it all!" "Look out for number one."

We might even draw our own map as we go along. But we are following a map, and like most dads on a family vacation, we rarely stop to ask directions.

While it is relatively easy to concede as true the notions of the hunt and the map, it is somewhat more difficult and painful to see the costs involved.

The hunt, no matter what map we follow, is a costly endeavor. It demands our money, time, energy, passion—indeed, our lives. When all is said and done, the hunt, wherever ours should lead, costs us everything. The only question remaining to be asked is, "Was it worth it?"

The mark of a successful treasure hunt, Jesus says, is joy. Maybe he is trying to tell us that joy is the treasure we are all trying to find.

Joy hidden in the seemingly barren field of our lives.

Joy tucked away in the hall closets and glove compartments of our everyday decisions and relationships.

Joy so buoyant and inexhaustible that selling the ranch seems like a bargain.

The kingdom of heaven is the treasure that brings such joy. The kingdom is not about attaining personal goals of wealth, status, fame, or leisure. Such things do not bring joy. The kingdom is about investing the resources of our lives in something far greater than ourselves. It is about pouring our lives

out in the costly and sometimes painful effort to
love the world God loves. It is about allowing ourselves to be used to bring joy, not to ourselves, but
to others.

A lady I know has found such joy. She has all the
comforts and opportunities that money can buy. But
she does not find her joy there. Each of the last two
summers she has joined our student mission team in
traveling to the Dominican Republic to help build
an orphanage for poor children. While there she
works as a nurse, caring for little sick children,
cleaning pus-filled sores, and staying up nights with
any of our students suffering from attacks of third-
world gastrointestinal bacteria. It is there, dirty,
sweaty, on her knees, caring for a Dominican child,
that my friend finds joy.

Such joy is ours only when we find the treasure of
the kingdom.

Jesus is the map.

Believing in Jesus is only a start. We must follow
him. The treasures of the kingdom are found, not
with the head, but with the feet and the hands.

CHAPTER SIXTEEN

A HARD BLESSEDNESS

And he began to teach them, saying:
Blessed are the poor in spirit, for theirs
is the kingdom of heaven.
Blessed are those who mourn, for they will
be comforted.
Blessed are the meek, for they will inherit the earth.
Blessed are those who hunger and thirst for
righteousness, for they will be filled.
Blessed are the merciful, for they will be
shown mercy.
Blessed are the pure in heart, for they will see God.
Blessed are the peacemakers, for they will be
called sons of God.
Blessed are those who are persecuted because of
righteousness, for theirs is the kingdom of heaven.
Blessed are you when people insult you,
persecute you and falsely say all kinds of
evil against you because of me.

5:2-11

The hero of the story lies limply on the bed. His name is Westley. His adversary, the despicable Prince Humperdinck, has had him tortured until he is "mostly dead." But as the evil prince enters his room to finish him off, Westley musters all his strength and manages to stand, draw his sword, and point it squarely at his mortal enemy.

"To the pain!" he declares defiantly.

The prince looks confused. "To the pain? I don't believe I'm familiar with that phrase."

Westley had earlier delivered a surprisingly serious line for such a silly movie. "Life is pain," he said to Princess Buttercup. "Anyone who tells you differently is selling something."

The scenes are from *The Princess Bride,* a film that happens to be not only silly, but surprisingly entertaining. Westley's challenge to the prince, in addition to being surprisingly serious, happens also to be true.

Many of us, I fear, have been sold a false bill of goods. Jesus has been marketed like aspirin. "And just bless us this day, Lord. Amen." Take him twice a day and hope, by way of blessing, he spares us the pain of living.

After all, that's what blessing is, right?

Having a "good day."

Things coming out OK.

Finding a parking space near the mall entrance.

Now there is certainly nothing wrong with trusting God with the minutiae of our lives. But there is danger in limiting God's blessing to those days when all the lights are green and all the news is good. We are led subtly, or not so subtly, to believe that if we can't testify to being the recipient of some form of "blessing" from Jesus, then something must be wrong with us, with our faith, or both.

Unfortunately, or fortunately, Jesus locates blessing somewhere on the other side of the tracks. Take a moment to read his words as recorded in Matthew chapter 5. Read them slowly.

Blessed are the poor in spirit.

Blessed are those who mourn.

Blessed are the meek.

Blessed are those who hunger and thirst for righteousness.

Blessed are those who are persecuted.

I don't know about you, but I rarely find myself asking for such blessings. Jesus' blessing is not identified with material wealth, physical health, or things that come out OK. Blessed, Jesus says, are those who struggle, suffer, and strive—the poor in spirit, those who mourn, those who hunger and thirst for righteousness.

Blessed are you when things don't come out OK, when the biopsy is positive, when you are ridiculed

for standing for what is right, when you pass up a
seductive invitation on behalf of purity, when your
longing for peace and justice puts you at the mercy
of the merciless. It's a hard blessedness—or a
blessed hardness.

The ugliest four-letter word in the English language, for most of us late-twentieth-century North
American types, is *pain*. We avoid even mild forms
of it like I avoid brussels sprouts. We have come to
assume that as North Americans we have the
inalienable right never to experience pain. We are
tempted to think God's main job description is to so
manage his universe that we never come face to face
with "the *p* word."

When pain intrudes as a most unwelcome guest,
we are likely to fall on one of two beds.

We can deny it:

Our pride and insecurity will not allow us to
admit the we hurt. So we suck it up, set our jaw,
and hope our smile doesn't look too much like a
grimace.

Or we become depressed:

We feel betrayed and abandoned by God. We've
gone to church, we've prayed, we've held up our
end of the deal reasonably well. Where's the blessing? Where's the return on our investment?

Jesus isn't selling us a false bill of goods. He
doesn't promise that we will never know pain and
struggle. He doesn't tell us we're defective if we
hurt. Rather, he promises blessing in the midst of
it all.

"In the world you will have trouble," he says ominously in John 16. Jesus lived on this side long enough to know that friends, brothers, and children die young. That the powerful feed on the flesh of the weak. And that to love greatly means to suffer greatly.

Blessed, he says, are the broken ones who have no words for their prayers.

Blessed are those from whom the weight of life's cruelty has crushed all breath, but whose last whisper groans what could be a prayer.

Blessed are they, for theirs is the kingdom, for they will be comforted, for they shall see God.

Blessed, in other words, are you.

Blessing is, says Jesus, not the avoidance or denial of pain and hardship, but the redemption of it.

We are blessed when, in our suffering, we are not alone. We are blessed when, in the storm of pain, his presence brings peace. We are blessed when, in the empty silence of doubt, we hear his quiet voice. We are blessed when, our eyes blinded by tears, our heart sees his face.

"In the world you will have trouble, but take heart, I have overcome the world." The hard blessedness of Jesus overcomes the world.

My world.

Your world.

CHAPTER SEVENTEEN

JUST DO IT

When they had gone, an angel of the Lord
appeared to Joseph in a dream. "Get up," he said,
"take the child and his mother and escape to
Egypt. Stay there until I tell you, for Herod is going
to search for the child to kill him."
So he got up, took the child and his mother during
the night and left for Egypt.

2:13-14

He was an ordinary man. The small woodshop he owned wasn't much, but then again he didn't need much. Just enough to make a home for his new bride and a future family. He was engaged to be married. He was an ordinary man.

His name, of course, was Joseph.

An ordinary man swept up in a whirlwind of extraordinary events.

His bride-to-be was pregnant. He was angry. He was confused. He was very sad. The wedding was still months away, and his beautiful Mary, whom he had never touched in that way, was already getting sick every morning. When she broke the news to him she claimed to still be a virgin—and something about the child being a gift from God. All he knew was the baby wasn't his, and that word was spreading around town like a virus, and he had some decisions to make.

Have you ever thought about Joseph?

Ever tried to climb into his sandals?

So often, as we watch yet another year's Sunday school Christmas pageant, we overlook the silent, nearly invisible character of Joseph. We smile in recognition of the little wise men in their terry-cloth bathrobes, the angels with tinfoil wings, and the obligatory papier-mâché sheep, cows, and donkeys. But the spotlight is always on the girl with the shawl pulled up over her head, looking wistfully at the Cabbage Patch doll in the cardboard manger.

We hardly even notice the quiet figure watching from the shadows.

The story, even when played by first graders, is moving. But Joseph is usually overlooked. He has no lines to recite. His part seems superfluous and ordinary.

Think again.

Joseph just might be the hero.

Joseph is heroic in the Christmas story for two reasons: When his world started to crumble, he listened. And when he heard the voice of God, he obeyed.

He could have divorced her.

He could have made her the object of public scorn.

He probably could have had her stoned.

His onetime friends in Nazareth were having a field day with this one, and that's for sure. Conversations became silent as he approached, and came alive with muffled snickering when he passed. It was humiliating enough to have people know she was pregnant, but even worse that she claimed to have never been with a man.

What did Joseph do when life was coming apart at the seams, when personal anguish and dreaded decisions soaked his sheets with sweat on cool nights?

He listened.

Would I have listened had I been in Joseph's shoes?

Hardly—I would have had too much to say:

"How can this be happening to me?"

"I didn't ask for this."

"Is it asking too much to have a simple, ordinary life?"

"I deserve better than this!"

Sound familiar?

If Joseph asked those questions, they aren't recorded. But we do know that he listened. He listened for some clue as to what he should do. A voice on which to hang his decision. And he heard.

"Don't be afraid," the voice says in the night, "to take Mary as your wife, for that which is conceived in her is of the Holy Spirit." The angelic messenger goes on to inform Joseph the child will be male and picks out a name for him as well.

Again, if I were Joseph, I may have said, "Easy for you to say she conceived by the Holy Spirit, but try telling that to her mother, or to the guys in the synagogue!"

Or perhaps, "OK, I'll do it. But do me a favor: At least let us pick out a name!"

Not only does Joseph listen when the crisis was deafening. Not only does he refrain from the questions and demands I would have found quite justifiable. But Scripture tells us he obeyed.

When Joseph woke up, he did what the angel
of the Lord had commanded him.
Matthew 1:24

If you were Joseph, how would you be feeling
about now? You've managed to hear and obey the
voice that tells you to believe the unbelievable, to
accept the unacceptable, and to do what is impossible. Wouldn't you be thinking you deserved to be
left alone for a while? You've gone beyond the call
of reason. You're an ordinary man; all you want is a
quiet ordinary life with your somewhat premature
little family. Please!

The voice speaks again. Just about when things
have settled down. The stares and twitters have all
but stopped. Life has once again taken on a happy
routine. And the voice comes again.

This time it says, "Get up! Get to Egypt! The
king is after your son."

"Egypt?"

"Now?"

"Why?"

Boy, would I have given that angel an earful this
time:

"Why would anyone want to hurt my son? That's
crazy."

"Egypt? Why not Palm Springs?"

"Now's really not a good time. It's 3:00 A.M., for
crying out loud!"

But Joseph's response is the same.

*So he got up, took the child and his mother
during the night and left for Egypt.*
Matthew 2:14

Joseph was an ordinary man caught up in extraordinary events. Events he didn't ask for. Events he
didn't cause. Events flying at him like linebackers
sacking a quarterback. The impact rattled his teeth.
What would he do? What *could* he do? How could
he face another day?

Maybe you, like Joseph, have spent more than one
sleepless night wondering what in the world to do
with circumstances life dropped on your doorstep.
Not only have you been in his sandals, you've worn
out a pair or two . . . or three.
    What did Joseph do?
    He listened.
    He heard.
    He obeyed.
    A prominent athletic shoe company has achieved
fabulous success (if you consider it successful to per-
suade teenagers to buy $125 sneakers) by marketing
their shoes with the phrase "Just do it." They have
managed to capture the discipline and commitment
of the athlete in training in three short words.
    You want to have biceps like Arnold
Schwarzenegger?
    Just pump some iron.
    You want to run like a marathon champion?

Just lace up those shoes (preferably Nikes) and run ten miles a day.

Just do it.

Now the answers to life's problems are not nearly as simple as the commercials suggest. But there is a kernel of truth hidden behind the marketing savvy. There are things in life, no matter how hard you try, you simply can't control:

The weather.

Your ancestry.

Your husband's drinking.

And there are things in life you *can* control:

Your tongue.

Your integrity.

Faithfulness.

When Joseph found himself in a situation beyond his control, he listened until he heard the voice of God. Then he obeyed. He coped with the uncontrollable by controlling the controllable.

In all the seemingly haphazard flux of life, there is precious little firm ground in which to anchor our tent pegs. But of God's desires we can be sure.

God wants our worship, our hearts, our minds.

He wants our behavior to be holy and pure.

He calls us to love our families, our neighbors, and even to find ways to act in loving ways toward our enemies.

He calls us to give ourselves away for the sake of others and to value relationships with him and our loved ones more than jobs and material possessions.

"Just do it," he says.

Joseph is the hero of the story because he obeyed. He did it when it didn't make sense. He did it when he had plenty of reasons not to. And he did it *now.* Maybe Joseph knew the key to turning an ordinary life into an extraordinary life was obedience. Maybe that's why God trusted Joseph as Jesus' earthly father.

Next time you find yourself in Joseph's weather-beaten sandals, try listening.

Listen hard for the voice of God.

When you hear it (and you will), obey.

It's not an easy answer. On the contrary, obedience is difficult. Just ask Joseph. But it also happens to be transforming. Obedience transforms the ordinary into the extraordinary—in Joseph, in me, and in you.

CHAPTER EIGHTEEN

DISTURBED

After Jesus was born in Bethlehem in Judea,
during the time of King Herod, Magi from the east
came to Jerusalem and asked, "Where is the one
who has been born king of the Jews? We saw his
star in the east and have come to worship him."
When King Herod heard this he was disturbed,
and all Jerusalem with him.

2:1-3

The dream was disturbing. I'm not one to recount vivid, exotic dreamscapes every morning, but this one I remembered. And it disturbs me still.

In the dream I was suddenly awakened (a curious twist of dream logic that makes it difficult to discern dream from reality) by an overpowering sense of anticipation. As I lay on the bottom mattress of a dorm-room bunk bed, a furious rush of adrenaline surged through me. Anticipation laced with sheer dread—like waking up in the middle of a 10,000-foot free-fall—led me to stare wide-eyed into the darkness at the foot of my bed.

I knew exactly what was causing my heart to pound. Jesus was about to appear at the foot of my bed. I knew, with the surreal clarity only dreams can provide, that Jesus stood in the hallway that separated the kitchen from our bedroom. It was like I could feel his presence preceding him through the doorway. But, strange as it seems, that wasn't what had me sweating bullets. Rather, it was the fact that I knew he was going to ask me to do something that disturbed me. I didn't know if I could stand hearing it. I didn't know if I could say yes. I wanted to run and hide.

Then, as I lay there, wanting desperately to both

see and not see Jesus, to know and not know his
request, I felt him speak to me. His voice was gentle
but very firm.

"I want to ask you to do something—but because
you are so afraid I will not ask you now."

And he left. The electrifying presence simply
faded away. And I lay in the quiet darkness of
another night. Disturbed.

> *Magi from the east came to Jerusalem and
> asked, "Where is the one who has been born
> king of the Jews? We saw his star in the east
> and have come to worship him."*
>
> *When King Herod heard this he was dis-
> turbed, and all Jerusalem with him.*

A star shines brightly in the night. A child is born
in a lowly stable. The whole world is disturbed.

The magi were disturbed. One can imagine them
clad in robes and turbans, their ancient observatory
filled with amulets, crystals, and primitive star
charts. Late one night as they peer into the black-
ness that is their lives they see a disturbing thing. A
new star! Jubilant shouting dissolves into serious
debate. Their profession is discerning the meaning
behind the movements of heavenly lights; what
could this astounding new thing mean? Whatever it
was, it had to be big. Really big. By the first light of
dawn they decide, crazy as it may be, to follow that
star—however far, whatever the cost—for they had
to know what, or who, it signified.

Herod was also disturbed. Fearful of the Romans
and hated by many Jews, Herod was by no means a
secure and happy man. One can imagine him, fat
and paranoid, gagging on his wine when he hears
the news of foreigners in town to worship a newborn king. "Preposterous! Ludicrous! I'm the king
of the Jews. Those idiots are following a pipe
dream."

Still, if it were true, it was disturbing indeed. A
new king would mean the end of Herod's egomania-
cal and ruthless rule, the end of his profligate life-
style, and quite possibly the end of him. It would
mean, at the least, there would be a power and
authority greater than himself. It was a possibility,
no matter how remote, he could not bear to accept.
The only option open was to kill that possibility.

All of Jerusalem, Matthew writes, was disturbed.
Not because a previously unknown supernova had
been discovered; not because a bunch of oriental
astronomers were making headlines; but because
the mournful wails of weeping mothers tore at their
hearts. The slaughter of the innocents. Herod, seeking vainly to ensure he would never have to bend
his knee to another, unleashed his murderous rage
on the children of Jerusalem. Little boys were being
buried by the score. Their mothers cried.

The coming of a new king, the coming of Jesus, is
disturbing. He disturbs us because he challenges us,
like the magi, to end our endless search for meaning
and get up from our familiar places and follow him.

He disturbs us, like Herod, because he confronts us as a power and authority greater than ourselves. We can no longer assume that we are masters of the universe, or even kings of our own lives.

The dream disturbed me and disturbs me still. Why was I so afraid? Was I afraid of what he might ask me to do? Would it have cost too much or been too hard? In all my praying to "know God's will," did I really not want to hear any answers but my own? Of all I do not know or understand about that dream, if it was a dream, I do know this. I was right to be disturbed.

Jesus intends to disturb us. He does not want to be just another shrub on the landscape of our lives, another still life hanging on the wall of our hearts. He stands and knocks. He wants to inundate our hearts and lives in a cascading tidal wave of love, a consuming fire of forgiveness, to be a conquering King.

Jesus, the child in the manger, the man on the cross, the living Spirit standing at the door of our lives, claims to be King. He forces a choice. Follow me with everything you are. Or try to kill me.

Either way, Jesus is disturbing.

What we do with that disturbance makes all the difference.

CHAPTER NINETEEN

THE BROKEN WINDOW

*Some men brought to him a paralytic, lying
on a mat. When Jesus saw their faith, he said to the
paralytic, "Take heart, son; your sins are forgiven."
At this some of the teachers of the law said to
themselves, "This fellow is blaspheming!"
Knowing their thoughts, Jesus said, "Why do you
entertain evil thoughts in your hearts? Which is
easier: to say, 'Your sins are forgiven,' or to say,
'Get up and walk'? But so that you may know that
the Son of Man has authority on earth to forgive
sins...." Then he said to the paralytic, "Get up,
take your mat and go home." And the man got up
and went home. When the crowd saw this, they
were filled with awe; and they praised God, who
had given such authority to men.*

9:2-8

"Ninety-four, ninety-five, ninety-six," the seven-year-old boy counted out the nickels, dimes, and pennies he had stashed in his money jar.

Ninety-six cents.

He hoped with all his might it would be enough to stop his so-called friend's tattling tongue.

As soon as the last *tinkle* of shattered glass had turned to silence, the boy's older friend plunged his traitor's dagger straight to the heart.

"I'm going to tell your dad you broke the window."

Anything, ANYTHING but that.

"Please don't tell my dad."

"Whaddaya gimme not to?"

"Money. I have money in my jar upstairs."

"How much?"

"Almost a dollar."

"Lemme see it."

Ever since his dad had received calls from neighbors about rocks bouncing down their roofs and clanging into gutters, the rule had been absolutely no rock throwing.

That time it had been innocent. The boy had just discovered he could throw rocks over the trees in the backyard, and it never dawned on him the rocks had to come down somewhere, such as on the rooftops of houses, or on cars parked in driveways, or on mothers in the act of hanging out laundry. His dad believed him, so there was no punishment— only a very serious face and a more serious rule.

No rock throwing.

But this time was different. There would be more than a serious face. There would be punishment. The sound of breaking glass was bad enough, but the sound of a leather belt zipping through belt loops in preparation for a spanking was more than he could bear.

How could it have happened? He and Bobby (the older friend) had been playing in the driveway. The driveway was full of small rocks. The distance to the garage was just about the distance from a pitcher's mound to home plate. One thing led to another, and the very first rock he threw broke a small pane in the garage door. An inadvertent bull's-eye from sixty feet. A one-in-a-million shot. On the first throw.

He knew the rule.

No rock throwing.

He knew he was in trouble.

Then his eleven-year-old "friend" blackmailed his life savings from him.

That would keep him quiet. But it wouldn't fix the window.

The gaping hole was still there.

His dad would surely see. He would surely ask.

So the boy decided to lie.

"No lying" was now added to "No rock throwing" as absolute rules he had broken, along with a windowpane, in one day.

He felt very bad. He was broke. He had lost a friend. When he lied about the broken window, something was broken in him, and something was broken between him and his dad, who believed him.

He felt guilty and very ashamed.

We don't know who the man was. We aren't told how long he had been a paralytic. We don't know how he came to spend his life on a mat. Did he contract polio as a child? Was he born that way? Did he break his neck or back in a bad work accident? We don't know. But we do know he had some good friends, and that those friends brought him to see Jesus.

What do we know of these men? How long had they known their invalid friend? How long had they known Jesus? Did their paralyzed friend ask them to take him, or did they insist over his objections and literally drag him through the crowd? What did they think Jesus would do for him? Had they seen him heal others with similar problems? We don't know. But we do know they brought their lame friend to Jesus, who was impressed by their faith.

One can imagine the scene. Four men, standing in front of the teacher, sweating from the effort of carrying a grown man through the crowd (or, as Mark tells it, from hacking a hole in the roof of a home and lowering him to see Jesus). A man lies in a heap on a mat, half covered by a tattered blanket. His

eyes are downcast and ashamed. The faces of the
friends are filled with desperate hope.

The elbowing crowd becomes still, and people
back off to give them room. A hush settles in as
they wait for the teacher's response.

"They carried him all the way here."

"Move over, I can't see."

"Shhh. . . . He's going to say something."

"*Shhhhh!*"

Into that silent expectation, and to that desperate
hoping, Jesus speaks. But what he says surprises
everyone.

"Take heart, son; your sins are forgiven."

"Wha'd he say? Wha'd he say?"

"*Shhh.* . . . I couldn't hear."

"I think he forgave his sins."

"Forgave his sins? What kind of a thing is that to
say?"

"*Shhh!*"

Indeed! With a broken man lying in front of him,
Jesus speaks not to his legs, or back, or neck, but to
his heart. Unsolicited, unpetitioned, he forgives the
man's sin. At best, a curious thing to say. At worst,
horribly insensitive and blasphemous.

"No one forgives sin but God!"

"He's gone too far!"

The crowd is beginning to turn. The quiet hush
erupts into chaos.

"Who does he think he is?"

"That man needs a miracle—not forgiveness!"

"He's blaspheming! He's made himself equal to God."

"Stop pushing!"

"Down in front!"

"*Shhhh!*"

Jesus speaks again.

"Which is easier: to say, 'Your sins are forgiven,' or to say, 'Get up and walk'?"

We have good reason to believe that what Jesus was driving at with his unanswerable question was the popular rabbinic belief that all sickness was the result of sin—and that no sickness could be cured until sins were forgiven. A man like this was seen as being a sinner, so bound by the weight of his transgression as to be paralyzed. Only the forgiveness of God could loosen his shackled limbs.

Jesus had already spoken the words of forgiveness.

The man remained on the mat.

The crowd murmured, "Blasphemy!"

The man's friends were confused.

Jesus was not. He spoke once more into the confusion.

"But so that you may know that the Son of Man has authority on earth to forgive sins, . . ."

He turned his face toward the figure hunched at his feet.

"Get up, take your mat and go home."

And he did.

Maybe Jesus knew the guilt and shame that had left this man a paralytic. Maybe he knew that whatever miracles and healings the crowd needed from him, they needed to know the miracle of forgiveness. Maybe he knew that sin and guilt have a way of burrowing into a person's life, submerged in memory and conscience, and binding the heart with the icy numbness of regret.

Most of us do not suffer from physical paralysis. Some of us do. But all of us are paralytics in one way or another.

Paralyzed in our ability to love.

Crippled in our attempts to obey.

Lame in our efforts to find joy.

Lurking deep within our disabled heart, tightening its immobilizing grip, is the crippling shame and guilt of sin.

Maybe you have sinned. You have tried to deny it, forget it, ignore it, bury it. But still the shame and guilt clings and entangles—and squeezes the life from your heart.

Maybe you have been sinned against. You have suffered at the hands of greed, lust, cold hatred, or loveless neglect. You too lie on your mat, unable to even dream of ever again leaping up and dancing for joy.

Listen again to the strong voice of your Savior. "Take heart, my son, my daughter; your sins are forgiven. Take up your mat and come home."

Nearly twenty years had passed. The boy was now

a man. The window had long since been repaired.
But it remained broken in his heart.

From time to time he would think of it. The rock
leaving his hand and traveling in an incredibly per-
fect line toward the garage window. The sickening
sound of the pane shattering. The sinking feeling of
paying his last ninety-six cents to keep his friend
quiet. The sad realization that even ninety-six cents
didn't take away his guilt.

The boy, now a man, and his father, now a grand-
father, were talking as they traveled somewhere in a
car. The conversation turned to memories of a
house where they had once lived, with a garage in
back. Before he knew it, the sound of breaking glass
filled the car.

"Dad, remember the time the garage window got
broken—and I said I didn't do it? Well, I did. I even
paid that kid across the street ninety-six cents not to
tell you."

"Really? I don't remember that broken window."

The boy and his dad laughed and talked some
more, and the sound of breaking glass faded into
forgiveness.

And a heart was set free to run and dance.

"Take heart, son; your sins are forgiven."

CHAPTER TWENTY

NELSON'S MUSTARD SEED

*"The kingdom of heaven is like a mustard seed,
which a man took and planted in his field. Though
it is the smallest of all your seeds, yet when it
grows, it is the largest of garden plants and
becomes a tree, so that the birds of the air come
and perch in its branches."*

13:31-32

At nine months of age, Danny weighed five pounds. Nelson sticks his little finger in the air and says in his heavy Puerto Rican accent, "He was skeeny lika dees—lika olt man." A local doctor told Nelson not to waste any time or money on Danny because he would surely die from malnutrition or one of its killing side effects.

But Nelson and Sylvia Medina took Danny into their tiny orphanage and began to care for him. Soon afterward, Nelson was cleaning Danny after he had messed himself, and he noticed something strange in his feces. He hosed off the waste and found small chunks of foam rubber.

Danny had foam rubber in his stools.

Nelson thought he knew where they had come from. He waded through garbage and bony chickens for several blocks to the corrugated tin shack Danny had slept in at night with his mother and seven siblings. He asked to see the place where the children slept. It was an uncovered foam rubber pad, taken perhaps from an old sofa tossed out by a rich family, and sure enough, in one corner there was a place where it looked as if rats had gotten to it. But it wasn't rats. It was Danny. A little boy had been eating his foam rubber mattress at night out of hunger.

About nine years ago, the way Nelson tells it,
God called him to minister to the poor children of
the Dominican Republic. A successful businessman
for years in both the United States and Puerto Rico,
he had lost everything when a trusted employee
embezzled a year's taxes owed to the government.
Nelson got a bleeding ulcer, which almost claimed
his life, but from which he believes God delivered
him. It was shortly after his healing that he heard
God's call.

In his mid-fifties, having lost everything but his
home, with a wife who had not yet warmed to the
idea (although she did very soon after), he moved to
San Pedro de Macoris, Dominican Republic. He
didn't know what he would do, how he would do
it, or even where he would live. But he believed God
would somehow, sometime, provide the resources
for him to fulfill his call. And Nelson Medina knew
how to pray.

He took what he had, along with a mustard seed
of faith, and planted it in a dusty corner of the city
called Barrio Mexico.

A couple of years later he founded Hogar
Cristiano por Fe, The Christian Faith Home, in a
rented three-room, concrete-block home with a tin
roof. He began, with whatever food and medicine
he could scrape together, to minister to the needs of
children like Danny.

And his mustard seed began to grow.

Let me tell you something about Nelson. From
five till seven every morning, he and Sylvia kneel on

the floor of their small apartment and pray. Nelson has brown, lumpy callouses on his knees. He'll show them to you. He also has holes in his shoes. He doesn't own a car, and the pesos he could use on taxis he prefers to use to buy milk for the "cheeldren," as he calls them. He walks a lot.

The seed was growing, but Nelson had been given a dream. He walked the streets every day and saw the hundreds of children growing up without adequate food and medicine. More than that, he saw children growing up without love, nurture, and care. He saw children who never heard of, or saw, or felt, the love of Jesus.

His dream was of a building in the middle of Barrio Mexico. A big building. A place where not just eighteen or twenty children could come, but where hundreds could come for healthy meals and medical care, a place where they could learn they were loved by Jesus.

Six years after arriving in San Pedro, Nelson applied with Young Life International to have a work team of high-school students from the U.S. help build the dream. His request was granted, and a small work team arrived. My brother Joe was the leader.

The next year Joe got me to bring a group as well. Soon nearly a hundred young people a year were making the pilgrimage to San Pedro armed with picks, shovels, and compassion. A large concrete block building began to rise from the squalor of Barrio Mexico.

This winter the Hogar Cristiano por Fe will be completed. It will enable Nelson and Sylvia to minister to up to 150 children a day as well as keep full-time staff.

The mustard seed has become a tree.

Let me tell you something about Danny. He didn't die. Danny is now eight years old. He is bright and happy and as mischievous as an eight-year-old should be. Three of his brothers come to the Hogar with him every day.

And the birds come and perch in its branches.

Let me tell you one more thing. If the kingdom of heaven is like that—count me in.

CHAPTER TWENTY-ONE

CHARLIE

*"Take a guard," Pilate answered. "Go, make
the tomb as secure as you know how." So they
went and made the tomb secure by putting a seal
on the stone and posting the guard.*

27:65-66

*After the Sabbath, at dawn on the first day
of the week, Mary Magdalene and the other Mary
went to look at the tomb.
There was a violent earthquake, for an angel
of the Lord came down from heaven and, going to
the tomb, rolled back the stone and sat on it. His
appearance was like lightning, and his clothes were
white as snow. The guards were so afraid of him
that they shook and became like dead men.
The angel said to the women, "Do not be afraid,
for I know that you are looking for Jesus, who was
crucified. He is not here; he has risen,
just as he said."*

28:1-6

So the women hurried away from the tomb, afraid yet filled with joy, and ran to tell his disciples. Suddenly Jesus met them. "Greetings," he said. . . . "Go and tell my brothers to go to Galilee; there they will see me."

28:8-10

When they saw him, they worshiped him; but some doubted.

28:17

The year was 1974. Beanbag chairs and lava lamps were the rage. Dorm rooms were not yet filled with VCRs, CD players, and personal computers. Streaking was the reigning campus phenomenon. We were college freshmen living in a freshmen dorm. Charlie was on my floor.

Charlie was about 5' 4", with sandy blond hair and red-rimmed eyes. He was also the most profligate sinner I had ever met in person. I mean, Charlie was a party reptile. He cussed like a sailor (my apologies to sailors) and drank with a frat-house flourish. Marijuana smoke wafted underneath his closed door nearly every night until the wee hours, and he regularly had his girlfriend in for days at a time. They weren't studying. For some reason I also remember he was an English major.

Now Charlie also happened to be a nice guy. A good ol' boy. He laughed a lot, got decent grades, and seemed to have plenty of friends. But Charlie was about as far from being interested in Jesus as anyone you could imagine.

Pilate was tired. He had a splitting headache. It had not been a good day. His wife had spent half the night thrashing about like a drowning woman.

Breakfast was ruined by her incessant rambling
about how this Jesus character kept showing up in
her dreams.

Then came the disaster at the office. A pack of
wild-eyed religious fanatics were frothing at the
mouth to see Jesus crucified. For the life of him, he
couldn't figure out what the big deal was. He suspected he was being dragged into a political tempest
in a teapot. They were jealous; Jesus had offended
them with his popular style; they wanted him gone.
He knew the charges were trumped up, but it was
his teapot, and they threatened to complain to
Rome, and he couldn't afford another bad report to
Caesar. So he had the pitiful and probably innocent
man crucified.

He rubbed one hand over his face from his forehead to his chin—as if trying to squeeze the pain
from his skull. He barely heard what they were
saying.

"And he said—if he said it once he said it a million times—he said, 'After three days I will rise
again.' Of course it's crazy—not possible, but what
if his followers have a plan to steal the body and
make it look like he's, well, resurrected!? Then
you'll have a real riot on your hands—you should
put a guard on the tomb for the weekend—just in
case."

First they twist his arm to have a man executed
unjustly. Now they bother him with this. He just
wanted to go home, have a few drinks, and try to
forget the look on that man's face.

"Take a guard," Pilate said, signing the document angrily, "and make the tomb as secure as you know how." Getting what they came for, they left Pilate alone, if not in peace.

Since the Pharisees sealed the stone tight and deployed a phalanx of burly Roman soldiers to stand guard, men and women throughout the ages have tried desperately to keep Jesus in the tomb.

They laugh him off as an irrelevant myth.

They try to debunk him with science.

They try to kill him dead with skepticism.

Why such vigilance? Why such fear of a man "dead" two thousand years? Simple. Should Jesus be allowed to shed his burial shroud, get up from the cold slab of rock, and emerge from the dank tomb, he would emerge as the object of their wildest fears. A living Lord. Not a God we can conveniently put away because he seems old-fashioned, or because his teachings cramp our life-style, but a God who lives, speaks, holds the keys to life and death, and makes a valid claim on our lives.

So they killed him.

But he didn't stay dead.

So they put a guard at his grave.

But he didn't stay put.

A friend of mine thinks the Resurrection may have been nuclear powered. If you have the time, he'll tell you why he thinks so. It all starts, he says, with the Shroud of Turin. The shroud is a very old piece of cloth, which bears a mysterious image of a crucified man. The easiest explanation is that the shroud is a hoax manufactured by Christian fanatics to support the resurrection of Christ. Or possibly that it is the burial shroud of another crucified man. Furthermore, the carbon 14 dating method has established the cloth as being from the thirteenth century, at the earliest.

My friend, however, points out several problems. First, the image on the shroud is photographically negative. This means it had to be created by a burst of something like light. No such source of creating photographically negative images existed in the thirteenth century. It is also highly unlikely that it could be of a crucified thirteenth-century man—for crucifixion had not been used for executions for several hundred years.

That, my friend postulates, leaves one problem: the possibility that the shroud is genuine, but that carbon 14 came up with a very wrong date. This problem begs this question: Is there some event that can explain both the photographically negative image on the shroud and carbon 14 giving a erroneous date? Naturally, my friend is glad you asked.

The one thing capable of confusing carbon 14 is the presence of neutrons in the fabric. The one known event capable of producing neutrons in amounts sufficient to do this is a nuclear reaction. A nuclear reaction also can produce a flash powerful enough to leave photographically negative imprints of human bodies on rocks (Remember Hiroshima?) or cloth. Therefore, my friend concludes, the resurrection of Jesus may have been nuclear powered.

Who knows? Maybe such an idea is kooky. But it is fun to think about. I don't think he'd even mind if you had your doubts. After all, Matthew tells us, even after seeing the genuine article, the resurrected Jesus himself, some worshiped, while others had their doubts.

The year is 1987. Beanbag chairs and lava lamps are the rage only in resale shops and garage sales. I've long since worn out the college sweatshirt I bought as a freshman. While flipping through the monthly alumni publication, my eyes fell upon the following entry in the notes for our class of 1978: "Charlie Krohn ('78) and his wife will begin their first term with Wycliffe Bible Translators this fall. They will be serving in West Africa."

My old foul-mouthed, pot-smoking, profligate classmate, Charlie, had become a missionary. A Bible translator. That's when I remembered he was an English major.

I don't know whether the resurrection of Jesus was nuclear powered or not. But I know this. All the nuclear reactors in the world can't hold a candle to the power that erupted from the tomb, burned its way through two thousand years of history, and lit the fire that now burns so brightly in the once-darkened heart of my friend Charlie.

You can look at the shroud and come to many
interesting conclusions. You can look at Charlie and
come up with only one: Nuclear powered or not,
Jesus is alive.

UPON THIS ROCK

Therefore everyone who hears these words of mine and puts them into practice is like a wise man who built his house on the rock. The rain came down, the streams rose, and the winds blew and beat against that house; yet it did not fall, because it had its foundation on the rock. But everyone who hears these words of mine and does not put them into practice is like a foolish man who built his house on sand. The rain came down, the streams rose, and the winds blew and beat against that house, and it fell with a great crash.

7:24-27

Sitting in front of my humming computer, trying to formulate an appropriate conclusion, three conversations flicker across the replay screen of my mind. The images and words are fresh; they took place just today.

The concerned mother of a teenage girl pokes her head in my office door and wonders if she could have a minute. It takes less than that for her to tell me her daughter was arrested two days ago.

And the rain came down.

A lovely high-school senior tells me over an ice cream sundae that her parents are getting a divorce. She's been through one divorce already and wonders why it has to happen to her again. She was hoping to go to college; now she doesn't know. She feels like her life is ending.

The streams rose.

A quiet woman in her mid-forties wonders aloud, "I find myself asking, Why? Where was God on the night Michael was killed?" She is three months into the darkness that is grief, having lost her only child, at twenty-one, to a traffic accident.

And the winds blew and beat against that house.

One ordinary day. Three ordinary people. Three storms threatening. Sure, one seems more like a light squall, another like a passing shower, while the third rumbles with gale-force fury. Yet each is capable of knocking its victim flat.

Significant, perhaps, is what Jesus does not say. He does *not* say, "Blessed is the one who hears these words of mine and puts them into practice, for upon him the sun will always shine." He does not say, "Blessed are those who follow me, for theirs will be smooth sailing."

Jesus says, rather, that whether you are wise or foolish, follower or fool, the rain will fall, and the wind will blow and beat against your house.

My three friends know this to be true.

My guess is you know it too.

Maybe your storm has come in the form of an untimely death.

Or failure.

Or a fall into temptation.

Or rejection.

Maybe it hasn't been so dramatic. Maybe it has been the rust of ordinariness and boredom creeping its way across the face of your life. The wind blows, sending you clattering around like an empty tin can.

For Jesus the question was not so much, "Can you avoid the coming storm?" but rather, "When the storm finally crashes ashore, will your house stand?"

Matthew's Gospel is about ordinary people, called by their King to build the houses of their lives on his rock-solid foundation. A foundation that will not crack and crumble when the wind grows fierce.

A foundation made strong by the concrete of the King's love. A foundation dug deep into the King's truth.

When the rain begins to fall, when the wind begins to howl, when we are drowning in the sea of ordinariness, Matthew would remind us:

Ordinary people are the raw material of the kingdom.

Miracles begin with ordinary sacrifice.

When we feel powerless, pure lives are not.

When we don't know what to do next, obey.

Failure is not final.

Forgiveness is.

Jesus our King turns up where we least expect him:

In the crucible of suffering.

In the storms of doubt.

In the face of a child.

In the resurrected lives of ordinary sinners.

Jesus is the King. He is building his kingdom. He is building it in and through ordinary people like us.

May we learn to see him.

May we learn to love him.

May we follow him closely.

May we crown him King.

Amen.